What About the Rest of Us?

Frank MacKay

About the Author

Frank MacKay's career in public relations, entertainment and politics spans four decades and encompasses a diversity of fields of work. In 1985, at the age of 18, he published his first music publication, "Network", which fast became a hit among music business insiders, musicians and their fans. Throughout the next ten years, MacKay built a significant following in the music industry as a band and club promoter. By the age of 25, he had launched three nightclubs known as Dr. Shay's and managed entertainers such as Criss Angel and CJ Ramone.

In 1992, MacKay became active in Ross Perot's third party presidential run. MacKay was always an avid student of politics, and early in his career in entertainment he helped club-goers register to vote by the thousands. In 1995, he became a key organizer in the Independence Party and active in third party politics. By the year 2000, at the age of 32, MacKay became the youngest State Chairman of a political party in New York State history, and has since been elected as State Chair of the Independence Party of New York nine times. The Independence Party has grown significantly under his leadership – it is the largest third party political organization in the nation with more than 500,000 members.

His success in entertainment and politics has been widely reported; MacKay has appeared in hundreds of national, state and local publications and has developed a niche audience among young political activists.

Frank MacKay resides in New York with his wife and four children. He serves as a Member of the Board of Governors for the Touro Law Center, holds a Master's degree from SUNY, Stony Brook. He was also awarded an Honorary Doctorate in 2008 from Five Towns College for his accomplishments in business and politics. He has also served on the Board of Trustees of two other New York colleges.

MacKay is the host of the television show, Turning Point with Frank MacKay and a daily radio show called Breaking it Down. The nationally syndicated talk shows highlight a range of topics from politics to pop culture. MacKay has conducted more than 500 interviews since 2012.

MacKay is the author of three books and has a large social media presence.

Email may be sent to Frank MacKay at FrankMacKay@yahoo.com

Table of Contents

Preface

The purpose of this book is to educate the public, elected officials, candidates and future candidates on the values of the Independence Party of New York State and the emerging Independence Party of America movement.

Not too long ago, I was with a friend of mine who said to me that in his opinion, the Independence Party of New York State should adopt a platform with five core positions on social issues, and he went on to describe his positions and why the Party should incorporate those ideas into its mission statement. When he was finished, I asked him, "Do you realize you just gave me the national Republican Party platform? Let me ask you; how are you registered to vote?" He answered, "I'm a registered conservative but I have considered joining the Independence Party." I told him, "You are exactly where you should be." A few days later, I was talking with two women who explained to me why the Independence Party should take a stance on some social issues. I urged them to give me some examples and they rattled off four liberal issues. When I asked them the same question regarding party registration, they gave me the predictable answer, and one of the women went on to tell me that she has never voted for a Republican and never would. I explained to them, in my role as the State Chairman of the Independence Party of New York, that I felt they were exactly in the right political party to support their views.

The reason these folks tried to convince me to have the Independence Party adopt certain positions is because they were aware that we had come under some criticism from editors in the New York print media, and from some partisan politicians, about our lack of position on hot button social issues. As the Party has grown in numbers, a major criticism of some newspaper editors has been that we "stand for nothing." Our partisan critics have also stated that the Independence Party lacks a "philosophical core." This could not be further from the truth.

Our position is that candidates and elected officials should be free to tell the voters what their views are, without dictates from political party bosses, special interest groups and restrictive party platforms that may not reflect the truth about an elected official or candidate. We stand for honest dialogue with the American People and an end to empty political posturing and rhetoric that has long been fortified by the media, in collusion with the nation's two-party system. We believe our nation's Capital is a mass of dysfunction, as are many state and local governmental bodies, and it's largely because our elected officials have erected a smokescreen fuming with empty partisan rhetoric, while behind the scenes they direct most of their attention to fundraising, the interests of powerful lobbyists and other political power brokers. We believe that a non-partisan third major party is the most direct path to fixing our broken system.

Let me be as clear with our readers as possible: anyone with highly partisan views on social issues such as abortion, same sex marriage, school prayer or any similar issues need not worry about the emergence of a non-partisan third major party in America. There are two well-funded major parties who want you on their voter rolls. We're not interested in displacing the major parties, but there are millions of people out there with moderate and independent views who don't feel as strongly about typical partisan social issues as they do about fixing our broken government. These people have a home with the Independence Party.

All too often we have heard about candidates, especially those in party primaries, bending their views to meet the narrow tenets of a Party's platform in order to gain a political advantage over their opponents. Public officials and candidates should be free to talk honestly to the public and vote their conscience.

We believe that much of the dysfunction in politics is due, in part, to this kind of highly partisan maneuvering, fueled by inter-party battles under the guise of polarizing social issues, which has the effect of preventing reasonable compromise. However, there is a far more disturbing element to political gridlock in government. The People have been led to believe that inaction in Washington, and in many state capitals, is due to their representatives standing their moral ground against the opposing party, when in reality they have become nearly powerless in the face of wealthy special interests. Our elected officials in Washington spend far more time debating issues like 'who should pay for birth control' than figuring out how to pay back the billions of dollars they borrowed against the Social Security Trust Fund or from Medicare.

There are millions of Americans who will no longer stand for this charade, and they have lost faith in the major parties and their respective leadership. A new major party – a third choice – is what this nation needs.

The Independence Party offers a model for change; our simple and straightforward platform promotes political independence and "centered and pragmatic leadership." Our core values embody what it means to be a true independent and we have done away with all politically divisive and polarizing language in our platform. The premise of the Independence Party is that elected officials should be free to legislate and use common sense in governing, and shouldn't be tied to a partisan social platform that fails to honestly represent their views or that may run counter to the best interests of the electorate. They should be free to make budgetary, policy and legislative decisions based on sound reasoning and input from their constituents, not heavy-handed political party bosses or special interest groups. Ultimately, our goal is to attract an independent non-partisan candidate for president who has achieved a high level of success in the private sector, and is willing to run for the presidency as a political independent.

This unique individual will also be the vehicle for the creation of a non-partisan *third major party in America.*

This won't be an easy battle. I witnessed firsthand the downfall of the Reform Party, the factional infighting, and how and why that movement failed. However, I also know what needs to be done to build a new national Party, and as the Chair of the Independence Party of New York, an organization with more than 500,000 members, I have learned firsthand how to run and win elections. Any effort to create a third major party in America will require an army of savvy, independent-minded political operatives from around the country. This isn't a task for the grassroots or the political purists. It will be a candidate -- a unique and populist individual -- that will ultimately drive the process and inspire his or her troops to build the movement, and succeed.

My goal is to help win elections for those candidates we endorse. I'm not there to tell anyone how they should live their lives, raise their children, choose a mate or find religion. I'm also not inclined to intervene in policy areas once a candidate takes public office. I believe my job is done once a candidate finishes his or her campaign and enters the realm of governing or legislating. This is a strong departure from the typical politics of the two major parties in the United States, and in fact, the Independence Party has been criticized by the New York print media because of this stance.

Niccolo Machiavelli shocked the world in the early 1500s with his book, <u>The Prince</u>, because for the first time, someone revealed the true nature of politics. His writings stood in strong contrast to the moralism espoused by early political philosophers like Aristotle and Socrates. In fact, Machiavelli is famously quoted for saying, "Politics have no relation to morals." What he meant was there is a difference between the actions of political strategists and campaign operatives versus someone elected by the people and entrusted to manage government affairs. The lessons in The Prince are still relevant today. Certain elements of politics have no place in the governance of a democratic state, and yet I believe there is a role for Machiavellian tactics in winning elections. In order to elect an independent to the White House, we will need to fight fire with fire. The Independence Party may appear at times as engaging in "politics as usual," but I'll accept the criticism as long as we ultimately achieve our goal to create a third major party in America.

It's Independence Day

"There is nothing which I dread so much as a division of the republic into two great parties, each arranged under its leader, and concerting measures in opposition to each other. This, in my humble apprehension, is to be dreaded as the greatest political evil under our Constitution."

— John Adams
John Adams, letter to Jonathan Jackson, Oct. 2, 1789

There is a sacred idealism in American politics which has served the nation well through much of its history – from periods of war and peacetime, and through depression and prosperity. These values, embedded in the American Constitution, and steeped in global history, have carried through time and connected our cities, farmland, and mountain folk, the ideologues and activists, the purists, the protesters, political philosophers, union leaders, independent journalists, political leaders, think tank scholars, and local community activists and organizers. Some are interested in politics and others have nearly dropped out of the system, but every year on Election Day, they are corralled by major and minor party political committees who call and beg them to cast their ballots along party lines. Many of these citizens are skeptics – knowing full well that their vote will not lead to anything beyond the ordinary status quo. In some cases, their jobs may depend on the status quo; after all, to the victors go the spoils. Others are easily cajoled into showing up at the polls by friends or friendly phone bank staff, and still others truly believe in the tenets of their largely Democratic or Republican Party affiliations. But the believers – those with strong partisan political ties – have become the minority.

More and more, individuals are proclaiming their independence from party political labels. They eschew major party candidates or vote for them after careful deliberation. Collectively, "independents" are a mismatched, unpredictable and undefined group which is increasingly becoming a major political plurality in the American politic. These are swing voters and registered infrequent voters that the major parties, the Democrats and Republicans, have failed to impress or definitively bring into their camps.

As a group, they are characterized by a range of ideas and values on the political spectrum – from very liberal, to moderate to conservative. As such, their definition of leadership may impress or perplex: Ross Perot, B. Thomas Golisano, Jesse Ventura and Michael Bloomberg are among the better-known 'independent' political icons because they have had significant cross-over appeal. They are viewed as outsiders who are not controlled by major party political bosses. Their independence and disdain for toeing the party line is, after all, their badge of honor.

In neighborhoods across America you will often hear citizens proudly announce that they don't involve themselves in 'politics'. In some cases this attitude is mistaken for indifference, but as John Mayer put it in his hit song, "Waiting on the World to Change," it is not that people do not care, it is rooted in a belief that there is little this generation can do to change the current course.

> *"Me and all my friends*
> *We're all misunderstood*
> *They say we stand for nothing*
> *And there's no way we ever could"*

-John Mayer

Quite simply, many Americans now believe that their elected officials are the product of a corrupt system of political rewards that function as the antithesis of our capitalist, entrepreneurial and bootstrapping ideals. Politicians, they believe, are what sanction government bureaucrats to pay thousands of dollars over market rate for fixtures, vehicles, and nuts and bolts. Thus, to be "anti-politician" is a trend that has become deeply embedded in American culture. It is not that Americans distrust the institution of government; they are skeptical that their elected leadership can achieve their mandates. [1] Distrust of politicians' ability to follow through on election year promises is a common thread among average Americans, and as a result, many voting citizens of the United States choose not to exercise their right to vote.

There is validity to this belief. Politicians are by and large duplicitous and promise more than they can deliver by pandering to political party leadership and special interest groups to obtain votes, win endorsements and raise money. This concept was perfectly summed up by George Stephanopolous who once famously remarked on Larry King Live that President Clinton, "has kept all of the promises he intended to keep."

Candidates make promises they cannot keep due to the same motivating factors that drive "get rich quick" schemes and general economic behavior. In order to win a majority of votes and gain acceptance, politicians must adhere to the tenets of their political party's platform and make statements that will resonate with special interest groups that can deliver large blocks of votes and campaign cash. However, the noted similarities with more logical economic behavior tend to end

---

[1] The Skeptical American: Revisiting the Meanings of Trust in Government and Confidence in Institutions
by *Timothy E. Cook and Paul Gronke, Journal of Politics: Vol. 67 Issue 3, Aug 2005*

once a politician is elected. Successful politicians often break their promises, in particular those related to large government reform initiatives, and yet enjoy a tremendous re-election advantage year after year.

On the contrary, if a company were to release a new product that failed to impress, that company would manufacture less of the product or stop its sale altogether. That company may even go out of business if it failed to sell its product. This is commonsense supply and demand economics. Our government, on the other hand, continues to expand in leaps and bounds – in the most disjointed and wasteful manner. Irrational government expansion has taken place throughout 150 years of two-party control of the nation's governmental institutions, and it has grown so large and so unwieldy that the People have become apathetic. They simply believe they can't change the system. I would argue that our federal bureaucracy has become so large and disjointed that our elected leadership in Washington, DC have lost a significant amount of control over the management of government affairs and our tax dollars. And it's not just on the federal level; I believe that many of our state and city governments have expanded in the same irrational manner.

We the People have to be able to rest some of the blame for this chaos with the two major political parties that have overseen the evolution of the bureaucracy.

Prior to 1930, the ideological differences between the major parties centered on fundamental issues related to slavery, industrialism, the gold standard and the sensibilities of war versus isolationism. Increases in federal spending and a shift towards more centralized control of managing the nation's economic affairs, following the Great Depression, led to deeper philosophical divisions between the Democrats and Republicans. The "divide" centered on what role the federal government should play in caring for its people through social safety net programs. It was during this time that the Democrats became defined as the party of the poor and the working class, and the Republicans reacted by defining themselves as proponents for states-rights and less national spending. As both parties sought to define themselves with the American public, and with the aid of a burgeoning mass media, a whole new dynamic emerged in the American political theater that has eroded peoples' faith in the power of their vote.

During the period following World War I, there was a distinct shift in the way news was reported to the American public. With more widespread distribution of the print media, political operatives from both major parties began to shape their "message" in terms of oppositional rhetoric in an effort to draw clear distinctions between the two parties and win support. This trend continues today, but it is even more destructive. The dishonest nature of major-party political rhetoric, widely distributed through mass media and the internet, has been one of the most destabilizing influences in the American political system to date.

What is political rhetoric? According to the Merriam Webster dictionary, rhetoric is defined as:
-   language that is intended to influence people and
-   that may not be honest or reasonable.
-   the art or skill of speaking or writing formally and effectively especially as a way to persuade or influence people.

As a political leader, I'm often amazed at the number of people drawn into heated discussions after listening to the latest rant on talk radio, FOX News or its equivalents on the left. I have come to realize that the divisive nature of the American political system has served the country well in many respects, and so has the media and technology in their own right, but the merging and modernization of the three forces has created a negative political environment that has eroded our democracy.

In order to reverse this trend, the People need to have the option of a non-partisan political movement built on principles and honest dialogue with the American people.

I believe that many elected officials are principled and have honest intentions when they seek public office, but they quickly become enveloped into the negativity of the system, which requires raising huge sums of money from special interest groups and engaging in dirty campaigns, based largely on false rhetoric, in order to gain the upper hand over their opponent.

As a fairly conservative spender, it is difficult for me to fathom how a political candidate, touting the need for after school programs for kids or a new park for a community, could on the other hand drop a few hundred thousand dollars on a media buy designed to do nothing more than lambast his or her opponent with partisan rhetoric. It seems wasteful and it doesn't make a lot of sense, but this is how our system has evolved. Sadly, it is only getting worse. Fortunately, many Americans see through the political posturing that take place in front of TV cameras, and can read between the lines of misleading political advertisements. These same people rightly distrust their news sources and the way mass media reports on politics. With oppositional rhetoric largely driving major party political discourse and the media and the internet providing the platform for the negative communication, many Americans, particularly political "independents," have become sick and tired of nasty political campaigns. They feel "bombarded" with false partisan messages, and more and more, they report that they are tuning it out.

Even so, political strategists and candidates have not let up. Superficial oppositional rhetoric has become so commonplace in American political discourse, and there does not seem to be an end in sight. It's like a disease festering through our political system.

Aside from political rhetoric, we are bombarded with twitter-like sound bites that are designed to capture our attention. For a political strategist, a successful "sound bite" is the reduction of a concept to a short sentence or two in order to convey a complex message. The sound bite was created by partisan political operatives and public relations professionals at the turn of the last century to tease the American public into wanting to learn more about the respective platforms of the major parties. It has since evolved from a teaser to an encapsulated philosophical statement on hot-button social issues designed to describe one party over the other, and often in disparaging terms.

For example, partisan voters who align themselves with a major party will often cast their votes based on a candidate's position on well-known hot-button issues, boiled down to political sound bites, that define their political 'side.' In a national election, this might include a stance on abortion ("Pro-life" versus "Pro-Choice") marriage ("Marriage Equality" versus "Gay Marriage"), government-funded national healthcare ("Obama-care" versus "National Health Care"), guns ("Pro-NRA" versus "Gun-Control"), and the list goes on and on. In local and state-wide elections, voters may seek out candidates who align with their opinions on issues such as tax rates, property rights and quality of life factors. The terms "Tax Freeze, Tax Cuts and Raising Taxes," are sound-bites thrown around quite often in local and national elections. Candidates naturally use these sound bites and other political jargon to pander to large voting blocks to win pools of support.

A politician that aligns with the Republican right is commonly marketed, in broad strokes, as 'pro-life' on the abortion issue, pro-2nd Amendment, and someone who is against gay marriage and Obama-care. A politician that is marketed as a Democrat is often promoted as pro-choice, pro-gun control, in favor of national healthcare and marriage equality. This is the common rhetoric and language that has

become embedded in the American political landscape over the last few decades.

The danger of voting the "party line" based on major party rhetoric and sound bites is that these positions may not even truly represent a candidate's actual social or political views.

In fact, flip-flops on many of these positions are well documented in political campaigns throughout the country, and in every level of government. Major party platforms do not always conform to the truth about a candidate because individuals running for public office don't always fit neatly into the strict tenets of a single political philosophy. This concept played out in most of the presidential campaigns in modern history. George Herbert Walker Bush had to abandon his pro-choice stance and his distaste for Ronald Reagan's conservative supply-side brand of economics in order to secure a place as Reagan's running mate. One of the most notable flip flops in history was roughly a decade later when then-President George H.W. Bush promised his Republican base "Read my lips. No new taxes." He raised taxes anyway, and couldn't recover from the flop. William Jefferson Clinton's running mate, Al Gore, from the conservative state of Tennessee, was pro-life during his early career as a Senator, and decidedly changed his public position to join Clinton on the Democratic ticket.

Furthermore, broad stroke issues tend to overshadow candidates' views relative to some of our nation's greatest infrastructural challenges; such as our fiscal stability, the national debt, road, bridge and levee repair, as well as tax, healthcare and safety-net stabilization. This is not to say that 'broad stroke' issues are unimportant, but it could be argued that voters are taking the easy way out when they cast their votes in line with these definitions of major party principles. And candidates often get a "pass" when it comes to solutions to the most pressing issues facing the electorate. The problem with sound bite branding of candidates and the overuse of political rhetoric is that American politics has become very superficial and downright dishonest as a result. These factors are the greatest contributors to widespread voter apathy and lack of citizen engagement, which then contributes to poor performance in many government sectors. These factors lead many people to question the values of the people who run for public office and become complicit with the dishonest nature of campaigning. It also raises concerns about their judgment in other areas of policy and lawmaking, as well as their ethical standards.

Once elected, many officials do in fact simply go with the flow of their political parties, because a candidate that can toe the party line, take their position cues from the pollsters and continue to lambast the opposing political party with false rhetoric will likely be guaranteed re-election. Politicians in Washington, DC, and in our state capitals, typically earn success by pandering to special interest groups that can raise hundreds of thousands of dollars for their campaign coffers, instead of by advancing principles and solving problems. Furthermore politicians typically advance through their respective ranks not due to their legislative skills, but more so based on their ability to raise money for themselves and others in their own political party.

Aside from raising money from wealthy public interest groups, major party candidates also raise a significant amount of money from individuals who are most vulnerable to their partisan political rhetoric. Here are some examples of deceptive letters based on typical polarizing rhetoric designed to raise campaign funds.

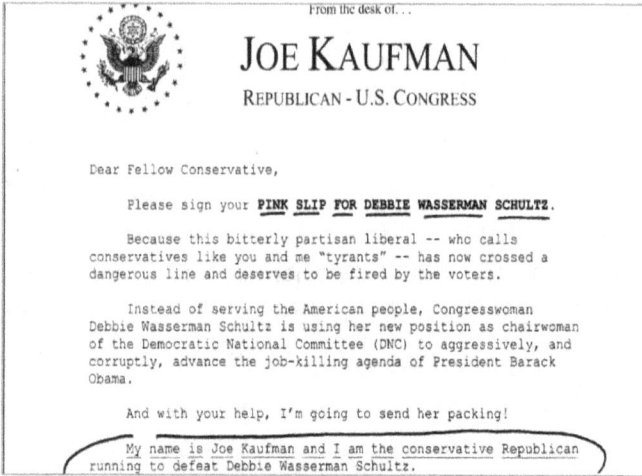

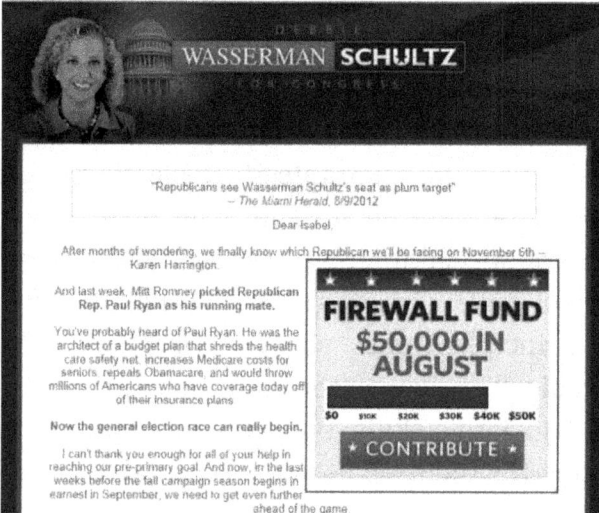

These are the kinds of campaign mailings sent out every day by candidates and political parties. In these particular mail pieces, a Republican running for Congress calls a Democrat a "job killer," and the Democrat accuses a Republican of attempting to throw millions of Americans off their health insurance plans. Both represent the typical jabs that one might hear during any given election season, on cable television or on talk radio, but there is little truth to either of their claims. This is major party rhetoric and it's largely based on exaggerated claims designed to scare partisan donors and voters into sending cash and casting votes. Not only are they misleading, but these types of campaign pitches often target senior citizens and veterans, who are among the most reliable voters and sometimes more vulnerable to these types of scare tactics.

The Independence Party of New York has also engaged in some of these types of mail campaigns, although not for fundraising purposes. It is fair to state that the negative tone of political campaigning is a systemic problem. I have personally taken a stand throughout the years by refraining from making oppositional statements against candidates we have not endorsed, and instead I have chosen to highlight the positive qualities of our candidates running for public office. The Independence Party can and should do more to raise the bar on the type of messages conveyed during political campaigns.

The time has come for political independents to take a stand against false and deceptive campaigns and fundraising pitches because it is damaging to our democracy, and it has a rippling effect on government. It has led to widespread voter apathy, poor accountability for elected officials, high taxes relative to services and poor performance in many elected bodies.

We now have a situation in which large pools of people have become desensitized to political campaigns; so much so that the incumbency rate in Congress has been greater than 90% in the last decade, and not because the public believes they are doing a great job. To the contrary, nationwide polls consistently report that 70% of the electorate believes Congress is doing a poor job! Most average Americans have simply come to expect that politicians exaggerate, and that newspapers and TV networks are biased but there is very little anyone can really do about it. Yet, regardless of their distrust, many citizens will go to the polls come Election Day for various reasons, and vote on the party-line that best represents their self-described brand of politics.

So what accounts for this illogical result? If our government were a product that failed to live up to its promise, most people would stop buying it.

One result of the system is, in fact, low voter turnout. Many moderates and independent voters in particular have been drawn into a large sector of the electorate known as non-voters or infrequent voters. Those who vote consistently tend to be strong partisans, and groups that are vulnerable to negative rhetoric, inherent in partisan political campaigns. This is why Americans need more choices at the polls.

Our electoral system has been so poisoned by decades of two-party political rule that it nearly ensures incumbency protection for both major parties through gerrymandering, restrictive state primary rules and polarizing rhetoric that discourages meaningful interest in politics. Many self-proclaimed independents have become disinterested and complacent with the status quo because they believe there isn't a viable alternative to the Democrats and Republicans, and year after year, politicians get a pass for poor performance.

Undoubtedly the first decade of the new millennium will hold its place in history as a period of mass uncertainty in the ability of bureaucratic structures to manage our economy, protect American borders, preserve peace in the world, and ensure steady employment for our growing workforce.

One of the greatest fallacies projected to the American public by the media and the two major parties is that gridlock in Washington is caused by both parties' failure to reach across party lines and work together to reform the federal government. The major parties claim to be 'polarized' on the issues, they claim to have steadfast "principles" and nothing ever gets done because the opposing party is the one preventing action on key legislation that could move the country in the right direction.

Truth be told: behind the scenes, throughout the Capitol and away from the media's glare, Democrats and Republicans get along pretty well. They talk, eat, play golf together and attend many of the same cocktail and holiday parties. They discuss regional issues, co-sponsor legislation and more often than not, are a part of the same small Washington clubs. Sure there are disagreements and some very profound disagreements, especially in relation to issues concerning military intervention and large social programs, but when it comes down to it, most are vulnerable to the very same influences; the press, campaign contributions and the insatiable desire to be a "player" among other powerful officials.

These forces represent the greatest challenge to the institution of government; the vortex of the nation's capital is a whirlpool of influence, money and power. The portrayal that policy making is often stifled by divergent beliefs and the lofty ideals espoused by the two major parties is largely a smokescreen that hides the realities of Washington's growing institutional ineptitude. Such an incestuous and destructive relationship exists between the two major parties, the mainstream media, special interest groups, and high-paid lobbyists in Washington, DC that any plans for grand reforms get lost in the midst of inter-party political posturing to maintain their comfortable status quo.

The result has been a systemic degradation of the federal government, which has been compounded by so many years of corruption and mismanagement that it is critically in need of a complete overhaul. It will take a special leader to take the system to task. The Democrats' roots have been sewn since Jeffersonian days, and Republicans have been major political players since Lincoln's 1860 victory. They have weaved a tightly controlled political structure on Capitol Hill along with the wealthiest corporations in America and influential special interest groups, and they will do anything possible to keep change – and independent leadership – from truly breaking their stranglehold.

The idea of a Democrat or a Republican running on a platform of "Change" as they take their cues from political captains and party leadership is a tough sell to the true political independent. Political independents know that unifying the Democrats and Republican will only increase their power to impede change, and the American people shouldn't fall for their attempts to co-opt the independence movement.

In short, Americans are clearly ready for a truly independent president and an independent movement, but what is lacking is a well-financed and charismatic political candidate willing to take on the task, and bring forth a third major party in America.

A Short History of American's Discontent with the Two Major Political Parties

In order to better plan for the creation of a third major party in America, it helps to look back at the history of independent movements in our nation's history, and their successes and failures.

There has been very little written on the subject of third party politics in America. Some may argue that apathy on this subject is justified. It was once stated to me by a professor of political science at the State University of New York at Stony Brook that third party politics is all but dead since the Reform Party failed to receive enough votes in the year 2000 to receive federal matching funds. People also make the argument that a third party vote is a wasted vote, but history reveals another side to the story.

Abraham Lincoln, one of our greatest presidents, was selected through the process of vote peeling in a four-way race. In November 1860, Abraham Lincoln of the fledgling Republican Party faced off against his Illinois nemesis, Stephen Douglas, as well as against John C. Breckinridge, the southern Democrat and John Bell, a former Whig party leader from Tennessee. Bell, Breckinridge and Douglass were all on the ballot splitting the Democratic Party to shreds while Lincoln was backed by a young but united group of former Whigs and others who had formed the Republican Party a few years prior to the election. In retrospect it is hard to imagine the

Republicans losing this race, but Lincoln won the presidency with slightly less than 40% of the popular vote.

It wasn't until 1912 that another third party run rocked a presidential election and changed the course of history. Theodore Roosevelt ran on the Progressive Party line, which was nicknamed the "Bull Moose Party". Roosevelt had run and won twice for the presidency in 1900 and 1904, and then threw his support behind Republican William Howard Taft in 1908. He eventually became disenchanted with Taft, and gave him a tough run in 1912 – much the same way that H. Ross Perot gave President George Herbert Walker Bush in 1992. The vast majority of Roosevelt's votes proved to spoil the election for the GOP, and turned New Jersey Governor Woodrow Wilson into President Wilson.

H. Ross Perot's United We Stand movement is probably the most notable third party movement in modern history because it was a major step forward for a candidate running outside the political establishment. Vote peeling from a major party candidate had the effect of swinging the 1992 Presidential election and changed the course of history. Perot dealt fellow Texas Republican, George Herbert Walker Bush, a fatal blow in the presidential election when he garnered nearly 19% of the total vote. This represented, by far, the margin of victory for Bill Clinton from Arkansas, but the race also inspired an entire political movement in the years that followed. The Reform Party of the United States and various statewide Independence Party organizations began to sprout up around the nation as a result of the excitement generated by Perot's strong showing that year. In Minnesota, the Independence Party was formed in 1992 by supporters of Ross Perot, and in New York, the Independence Party was formed as a result of billionaire businessman B. Thomas Golisano's run for Governor in 1994.

Gordon Black, who was Ross Perot's pollster and the author of The Politics of American Discontent: How a New Party Can

Make Democracy Work Again (Wiley: 1994), was Tom Golisano's first campaign manager. Laureen Oliver from Greece, New York, became the organization's first State Chair and has been Golisano's chief political advisor through the years. The Independence Party of New York certainly wasn't the first minor party to have a role in New York's unusual fusion system of politics, which is similar to a multi-party system, but it is by far the largest third party in the State's history, and likely the nation, with more than 500,000 members. I was elected State Chair of the Party in the year 2000, and I have been humbled to have the opportunity to lead the Party ever since. It's a vibrant and active organization, and our growing enrollment is not surprising given the average Americans' sense of distrust of the major political parties. More detailed information about the Party's history and excerpts from my LI News Radio interview with Laureen Oliver may be found in the next chapter.

By the year 2000, an often-cited Gallup Poll found that sixty-seven percent of Americans favored a strong third party that would run candidates for president, congress, and state offices and nearly a third of Americans polled indicated that they were self-described independents. This sentiment played out in the 2000 elections, where there was a high level of vote splitting among the American electorate. In that year, the United States Presidency was decided by a historically small margin of votes, and again, a third party candidate played a role in the outcome. Independent/Green candidate Ralph Nader went from being a heroic figure for his lifetime of consumer advocacy, to becoming the bane of America's registered Democrats. Nader himself gloated over "costing" Al Gore the Presidency. In the highly contested race where hanging chads became a household word and Florida's outdated punch card voting machines took the spotlight, George W. Bush was declared the victor by one electoral vote, but failed to capture the popular vote due to vote peeling by Nader and numerous other minor party candidates. Nader's role in the upset was parodied in a late-2004 episode of the Simpson's in which he was portrayed as a covert member of the Springfield Republican Party – and cheered by his fellow Republicans for his noble run. Needless to say, many Democrats were disappointed with Nader's role in the close election.

Ralph Nader had run on the Green Party line, in part, to defend America's left wing, and at the same time his polar opposite was claiming to do the same thing on the right. Conservative journalist Pat Buchanan, who for many years championed right wing causes, was especially popular with the country's religious right. Much to his dismay, the conservative stalwart garnered less than one percent in the election. That is far below the five percent needed in order to receive federal matching funds for the candidate's party. The low vote total may have seemed like a waste of time to many people, but the run would certainly have looked more significant if the Supreme Court would have ruled that Al Gore won by several hundred votes in the electoral-vote rich state of Florida rather than the reverse. In that case, Buchanan would have been crowned the spoiler rather than Nader!

The margin of victory in Florida for George W. Bush was so thin that any number of scenarios could have taken place. On the stranger side, had Nader not been on the ballot in Florida, the name Dr. John Hagelin could have been a new household name in America. Little known Hagelin was the titular head of the Natural Law Party, which is run and maintained by practitioners of Transcendental Meditation or TM. The Natural Law Party has a very left of center party platform and strongly preaches pacifism. If Nader had not been on the ballot in the Sunshine State, this small group of independents may have gotten the credit or blame, depending on the viewpoint. Regardless, having an impact on something as monumental as a

Presidential race is a public relations windfall for any independent movement. The Independence Party of New York ran Dr. Hagelin on its ballot line that year.

In the case of Buchanan, it is now clear that he was attempting to compete with Bush for the heart and soul of the Christian right. In retrospect, this appears to have been an uphill battle probably not worth fighting. One reason is that G.W. Bush is a born- again Christian. In addition, the former Texas Governor is a favorite among pro-life voters. Since there is such little room for someone to run right of Bush, Buchanan would have been better off sitting out of the 2000 election.

Buchanan got his first taste of candidate-*itis* when he ran against G.W. Bush's father in several Republican primaries. The short-lived success that Buchanan enjoyed against the older Bush was aided by a perception that he had handled the nation's economy poorly. Also, George Herbert Walker Bush was far left of his offspring, which created a larger ideological gap for someone like Buchanan or Pat Robertson to run on. The Republicans that were concerned about the economy could have banded together with the religious right in 1992, which would have been a better year for Buchanan to run an independent candidacy. Perot took votes from that combination instead. This is not to say that Buchanan would have gotten anywhere close to the 19% Perot hauled in. Perot spent $75 million dollars on his campaign, which was a shocking amount at the time.

While the seeds of political discontent began to blossom in the early nineties, by 2005, in the wake of Hurricane Katrina's destruction of New Orleans and the Gulf Coast, the public's confidence in the federal government to care for its own people had been badly shaken, and for the first time in decades, it demonstrated the carelessness in which we have managed our basic infrastructure needs. The poor federal response to Hurricane Katrina, and the fact that 1836 lives were lost in a matter of days, brought to light some serious failures surrounding the United States federal government and had people questioning how our tax dollars were being spent.

Decades of national fiscal irresponsibility hit the nation with similar force in the final years of George W. Bush's presidency, leading to massive corporate failures and high unemployment. International confidence in the dollar began to wane, and the economic and human costs of the war in Iraq were blamed squarely on the Bush Administration.

Bush's political fallout began to take shape in early 2006. Polls showed Bush with a mere 43% approval rating and with Americans stating 2:1 that the nation must move in another direction. It predicted upsets for Republican House Members too, with 55% of Americans citing their disapproval of that institution's performance.[2]

Elections for the United States House of Representatives were held on November 7, 2006, with all of the 435 seats in the House up for election. Democrats picked up thirty seats and defeated twenty-two Republican incumbents. It was the first time in history that Republicans won no seats previously held by Democrats in the House or the Senate.

In the Senate, Democratic candidates defeated six Republican incumbents, and no Democratic incumbents were defeated. Joe Lieberman of Connecticut won re-election as an independent after he lost a primary on the Democratic line. In Vermont, Bernie Sanders, also an independent, was elected to the seat left open by independent Senator Jim Jeffords. Both senators caucus with the Democrats.

The results of the election were rather predictable. The public's disillusionment with the cost and motive for prolonged wars in Iraq and Afghanistan were a major reason why Americans voted against Republicans. While the economy still seemed to be performing well through 2006, the middle class

---

[2] Los Angeles Times/Bloomberg Poll released 1/27/06

and working classes of the nation no longer believed they had been helped by the Bush tax cuts, and with health care costs rising at an alarming rate, and essentially squeezing the small business people to the hilt, many average working Americans lost hope in the promise of a "healthy economy" translating to more income for themselves. Rising prices at the gas pump also led to political disenchantment from all socio-economic sectors, and frustration in the year 2006 translated into the wallop against the Republican dominated Congress.

By August 2007, a USA TODAY/Gallup Poll reported that 58% of Americans believed the two major parties were doing "such a poor job" that a third party was needed. Just a third of the respondents reported they felt the established parties were doing "an adequate job of representing the American people."

In that same month, the Independence Party of New York published a series of articles on the direction the independence movement must take to encourage independent voters and potential candidates to take on the Washington establishment. On September 23, 2007, hundreds of independents from all walks of life and political persuasions gathered at the Crowne Plaza Hotel in White Plains, New York and organized the Independence Party of America. It was unlike any other event of its kind. Impassioned for change, the Party took a bold stand and initiated a plan to engage Americans in a new type of political dialogue, one completely devoid of the politically divisive social issues that mask the most serious issues facing our country.

Here is the statement issued by the new Party on the eve of its formation:

It is time we send a new political prototype into the White House -- a true non-partisan Independent. Someone who has led a successful life in the private or non-profit sector, away from Washington, and can drive

the type of innovation needed to repair its broken systems and regain the faith of the People.

Each and every state in the nation will soon represent the Independence Party of America.

The Independence Party of America will offer a 'third way' to professionally manage the federal government. As America's largest third party organization of political independents -- *with more than 350,000 members in our home state alone and growing daily* -- we intend to bring INDEPENDENCE to the national forefront in the 2008 race for the White House. We intend to change the DEBATE in 2008 and offer a viable alternative to the two-party duopoly. And we hope to recruit America's increasingly apathetic electorate with a plan and a mission to offer a REAL alternative to the major party candidates.

Millions of people across the nation have voiced their distrust of Washington's extreme partisanship -- and the growing incompetence that characterizes the federal bureaucracy.

Our great democratic system of governance has been corrupted by significant waste, fraud and mismanagement. While the largest corporations in the nation reap billions in profits from an unprecedented surge in federal spending, average Americans struggle to pay for their basic medical expenses, housing and energy needs.

All government spending is a tax on each and every one of us, and WE, THE PEOPLE must demand appropriate accountability. We deserve a better quality lifestyle relative to our contributed tax dollars. We deserve a better reputation on the world's stage relative to the average American's honest goodwill towards all people, and the sacrifices that many generations have endured to improve the lives of others around the

globe. We deserve competent, intelligent and forward-thinking leadership to lead the nation to new heights of prosperity.

As independents, we believe that America's choice for President will emerge from the grassroots with a platform to bring competent and revolutionary management principles to transforming the federal government. The Independence Party of America will be the great big tent for all voters - left, right and center -- to feel confident that we are on our way to changing course for the better.

The Independence Party of America didn't realize its goal to find a presidential candidate in 2008. As the Chairman of the Independence Party of America and New York, I am the first to acknowledge that we had, and still have, a tremendous task ahead of us, and there will be a lot of resistance along the way.

The Independence Party of America also wasn't the only political party seeking to ride the wave of Americans' discontent with the two major parties in the year 2008. Washington-based groups such as Unity '08 rose to prominence in the months leading up to the 2008 elections with calls to end the polarization in politics.

Another movement that had its roots in the 2008 presidential election has been more successful. The Tea Party movement grew out of conservative presidential primary candidate Ron Paul's political campaign which centered on eliminating the national debt, reforming government and reducing taxes. The movement has gained in popularity over the years, and is a banner of pride for the conservative wing of the Republican Party.

The public's disillusionment with the dismal state of the federal government was a strong factor in the 2008 presidential races. Barack Obama, a long-shot candidate in the early phases of the primaries, rose to pre-eminence by touting an agenda for "Change" and his message truly shaped the entire nature of the presidential election. John McCain, who many had written off early in the presidential primaries, came up from behind and won the Republican nomination for president because of his own maverick reputation and credentials. Both major party candidates appealed to independent swing voters. The Independence Party of New York threw its support behind McCain.

In the final days of the 2008 campaign, Obama sought to highlight his independent credentials by running Perotesque-style 30-minute infomercials on all of the major networks. In November '08, Democrats took both the White House and Congress with comfortable margins of victory.

The 2008 presidential campaign will go down as one of the most engaging in recent history and for a brief moment it left many Americans feeling more "hopeful" for the future of the country. Obama, a former freshman Senator, ran as political outsider, someone less entrenched in Washington's ways. He was the first black president in our history, which delighted the world as a groundbreaking moment, and for a relatively brief moment in time, America appeared visibly united as a country.

However, Obama's honeymoon with the general public was short-lived, and although he won re-election in 2012, the American jury is still out on Obama's ability to follow through successfully on his election year broad-stroke promises. As of 2014, a significant round of inter-party finger pointing and inaction has emerged relative to the American Care Act, efforts to revive the nation's economy, reduce the debt and raise the debt ceiling. Failures in military policy and violent eruptions in the Middle East have further eroded confidence; and Washington, DC continues to be viewed as an example of mass bureaucratic dysfunction and financial waste. Despite strong public opinion in favor of reform, there is continually no action on issues such as immigration, Social Security and Highway Trust Fund stabilization, or dealing with unemployment and the enormity of the national debt. Instead, Congress is now in the business of passing feel-good laws that help marginal constituencies that have almost nothing to do with its Constitutional mandate.

The ability to achieve the grand promises of Obama's catchphrase, "Change we can count on," has been stymied by systemic gridlock and by the President's failure to build the type of consensus the catchphrase implies. The two-party system has been so corrupted by the forces surrounding power that our elected leaders are essentially paralyzed to apply sustainable and meaningful solutions to the nation's real problems. The 2014 mid-term elections led to a Republican landslide in both the House and the Senate, as well as in gubernatorial races across the United States. This represented a stunning public rebuke of Obama's leadership. Americans desperately want change. Unfortunately, regardless of which party is in power, independents recognize that there will not be any significant movement on fundamental issues because it would take tremendous independent political will to deconstruct the bureaucratic mess. They don't have solutions and even if they did, the leadership to force change is sorely lacking. During the last two decades, the major parties have embarked on a strategy to convince the American public that the current inaction and gridlock is due to entrenched rightwing versus leftwing idealism. At its best, it's a political smokescreen, but one could also make the argument that it's a delusional excuse to mask long term political failure. If Americans truly want to stop the dysfunction, they will need to change the paradigm in the political landscape. That would mean a third major party in the country.

Our Founding Fathers envisioned a nation grounded in checks and balances, but what has arisen is a dangerous imbalance. The greatest impediments to reversing the current trend are the two major political parties and their control over the flow of trillions of dollars into projects and issues that are most important to their wealthy benefactors; well-funded corporate special interests, individuals with strong ties to foreign governments and the nation's major lobbying groups. These 'special' interests give generously to the major political parties, but along with these donations, they have achieved significant influence over party leadership and elected officials on both sides of the aisle.

Reforming the campaign finance system could possibly lead to less political gridlock, but it's unlikely that either of the major parties would support meaningful change, and many of the initiatives to restrict the flow of money into political campaigns have been successfully challenged on First Amendment grounds.

The only reasonable path to reform is through a viable third major party movement to counter-balance the current two-party system.

The Stone the Builders Refused:
The Independence Party of New York

The Independence Party of New York has a non-partisan, centrist and pragmatic platform that could be a model for change in the American politic and for a national third party infrastructure, but I have always said that a political party can't fully emerge without the right candidate for our time. The Party has experienced its share of growing pains, but it has also had a considerable amount of success since its inception. The Independence Party of New York is one of a handful of independence political organizations that grew out of Ross Perot's 1992 campaign for the presidency.

It was around that time that I, along with millions of Americans, began to take an interest in alternative politics. I was a nightclub owner and entrepreneur, and Perot's image as a successful businessman concerned with America's financial stability resonated well with me. I also liked his independent credentials, and as anyone who knows me can attest to, I was never one to follow down a traditional path.

In 1992, I got involved with Perot's first run for the presidency and I began to take an active interest in independent politics and party building. I was among the first people to enroll in the Independence Party of New York when it was officially established in 1995, and I was appointed to a local town chairmanship that same year. It was also around this time that I began to take an interest in the growth of the state party.

Laureen Oliver, of Greece, NY, was the first State Chair of the Independence Party of New York. She co-founded the party with B. Thomas Golisano, who was the Party's first gubernatorial candidate in 1994. Golisano's strong showing at the polls that year guaranteed the party's position on the New York State ballot in subsequent years, and laid the foundation for it to become the fastest growing minor party in the state's history.

It has also had its share of controversy since its founding, much of which was centered on the involvement of a group of individuals from New York City whom many people have described as cult-like followers of the late Fred Newman. Newman, the originator of a psychotherapeutic philosophy called Social Therapy, was also a playwright and co-founder of the Castillo Theatre in New York. He had a history of involvement in radical political movements and was reportedly behind the underground Marxist International Worker's Party, as well as the defunct New Alliance Party. In 1988, Newman's New Alliance Party ran African American activist Lenora Fulani for President, and the two remained very close political associates up until Newman's death in 2011.

It was in the year 1995, when I was in my late 20s, when I first became familiar with Newman and his band of political operatives, and I found it to be a rare and fascinating view of the inner workings of a radical 60's-type era political organization. As a New York City-based group, they had access to a cadre of foot soldiers who could carry out Newman's political strategy, which was clearly to take control of the new Independence Party of New York. With the aid of a close inner circle of savvy political operatives, namely Cathy Stewart, Jacqueline Salit, their attorney, Harry Kresky and fundraiser, Gabrielle Kurlander, they systematically registered a large number of people into the Independence Party's voter rolls. At the same time, they strategically began running and winning state committee primaries in areas of New York State with heavily weighted vote. By 1998, Newman's group had successfully garnered a significant share of state committee to have a seat at the table in choosing the Party's State Chairman.

Cathy Stewart, one of Newman's political operatives, was the individual primarily responsible for carrying out the group's political goals. In 1998 she cut a deal with the party's second elected Chairman, Jack Essenberg, to support him for re-election in exchange for his vow to give the New York City group local control over political endorsements. Soon afterwards, he would renege on the arrangement – a calculated error that would help lead to his ouster in February in the year 2000. That's the year I was elected State Chairman of the party, and I have held consecutive terms in office ever since.

I had the opportunity to interview Laureen Oliver in September 2014 for my radio show, Breaking it Down. With her permission, the interview has been transcribed below for this book. I was truly grateful for her time, and for all of the work she has devoted to developing an independent political movement in the United States. The interviewing was very revealing and shed some light on Tom Golisano's motives for running for Governor of New York and the tremendous role he has played behind the scenes in paving a future for a more diverse playing field for third parties in New York and nationally.

An interview with Laureen Oliver, Co-Founder of the Independence Party of New York State

Frank MacKay: I'd like to welcome everyone to Breaking it Down. Our very special guest today is the co-founder of the

Independence Party of New York, and a major player in the independent political movement in the United States. Laureen Oliver, welcome to Breaking it Down.

Laureen Oliver: Thank you, Frank.

Frank MacKay: I'm sure you have told this story a million times, but the Party you built, and what Tom Golisano built, along with others, is still going strong, regardless of our detractors. You were the original State Chair of the Independence Party of New York, and for reasons of full disclosure, this is the woman responsible for me being State Chair. So anybody who hates me can blame her for bringing me in!

Laureen Oliver: Frank, I want to congratulate you. I hear you are on your 14th year as State Chair. I didn't know anyone could go that long!

Frank MacKay: Well listen, thank you, but if not for you and Tom Golisano there would not have been a party. So let's start with you and get a little history on your life and start in politics. Tell us about your upbringing and where you grew up. What were your parents like and what were their political views?

Laureen Oliver: Well I grew up in Rochester, New York and I lived there for just about all my life until I retired. I grew up in a middle class Italian family in the city and then I moved to the suburbs. My father, and just about everyone in my family, were self-employed. My father was an electrical contractor, as well as owning a number of other businesses and rental properties. My father was also a devout Republican. I grew up in a home listening to the Sunday morning talk shows and to friends and family talking about and what was going on in the country. That is kind of where I got my start. Later on, when I got out of High School, and before I went to college, I worked for the State of New York as a jury summoner in what was called the Hall of Justice, which was where all the courthouses were. I learned a lot about politics there. I got to see what would happen every time a new administration came in to run things and how they would change department heads. Normally, they brought one department head in who didn't know anything and they would bring in another who didn't know anything because it had to do more with politics than their skill set. That was disappointing. And as I sat there and worked for five or six years before I went to college, I thought someday I would like to get involved in politics and change that.

Frank MacKay: So those were the early years, but I know you became a successful business owner after college. Tell us about your career and why you decided to enter politics.

Laureen Oliver: As I grew older, and I left the State job and went to school and became an accountant. I went into private practice and the bulk of my clientele were small businesses. I learned about the bureaucracy, and what small businesses would go through just to exist in a country built on small business. There was no lobbying organization that supported these people. You could be a thriving company and somebody would go bankrupt that was your major vendor and you went down with them. There was no protection. I kind of followed tax law as well as politics and I was never really impressed. Then like most of us, in 1992, I followed the Ross Perot campaign.

Frank MacKay: Perot had a lot of charisma, some quirks too, but he inspired a lot of people to think outside the two-party system.

Laureen Oliver: Yes, even though I was a little unsure about the messenger, I liked the message. Then 1992 and 1993 I decided to make a run myself for Town Supervisor in the Town of Greece, New York. Greece is a suburb of Rochester and it is the second largest town in the State. It had over 100,000 people. If it were a city it would be the seventh largest city in the State. I gave it a serious run. That's where I learned all about ballot access.

Frank MacKay: So you ran as an independent candidate, which meant you had to figure out how to get the ballot without the help of the major parties. That's not an easy thing to do, especially back then.

Laureen Oliver: Yes, I had to do my own petition drive. I gathered more signatures than the entire Democratic and Republican Party slates in that town combined. Everyone marveled that I could do it. It was a lot of work. I learned a lot about how to do a petition all by myself, and nobody sued me because I wasn't anybody at that time.

Frank MacKay: You weren't a threat to the major parties at that time, but that wasn't the case for very long.

Laureen Oliver: I ran for election that year and the powers that be in the Democratic and Republican parties were gambling that I would never get more than 5 or 6 percentage points. I turned around and got just about 20% of the vote. After that I became popular within the Democratic and Republican parties. They began to court me, but the more I watched what they were doing, I said to myself, I'm a square peg and I don't fit in a round hole.

Frank MacKay: So this was 1993. Were you working with Tom Golisano at the time?

Laureen Oliver: Well, simultaneously to that, and unbeknownst to me, Tom Golisano and Dr. Gordan Black were working together on something else. I ran in 1993, but in 1991, Dr. Gordon Black was the President and CEO of the Gordon S. Black Corporation, which went on to become the Harris Poll Company. Black was a political science professor who taught at the University of Rochester, but his love was independent politics. Gordon did a survey in 1991, which was funded by Tom Golisano, and found there was a great deal of discontent among voters of the Democratic and Republican parties. Even back in 1991, people thought our government and political parties were polarized. They took that survey and went onto C-Span, in the middle of the night, and they got something like 7500 phone calls over the next 2-3 weeks from people all over the country. So Tom and Gordon Black went on to form an organization which included a number of other prominent Americans, including Lowell Weikert, Jr. and others. There were seven people involved, and they tried to put together a national third party in 1991.

Frank MacKay: Was Ross Perot involved or was this before Perot?

Laureen Oliver: This was before Ross Perot. When Perot emerged, they waited to see what Perot would do. Perot didn't have an interest in a third party. His interest was his race for President in 1992. When they realized he wasn't going to get involved in third party politics they continued on. I ran in 1993, and that is about the time I met Tom and Gordon, who were from Rochester. They had brought a bunch of people together in New York and they thought they should start a third party. I had just finished my run for Greece Supervisor and finished right behind Ross Perot's 20% and so I was kind of the leader in the state behind Perot. So Tom and Gordon came to me, recognizing my petition drive, and asked if I could help put together a third party in the State of New York. At the same time, and by now it is late 1993, they were still trying to work at the national level to create a third party. The efforts on the national level had started to evolve a little bit, but it got robbed by Lenora Fulani. They had a big meeting in Arlington and they had people from all over the country come, and they were supposed to have delegates from every congressional district. She had bused in hundreds of people and gave them false IDs and made them from different parts of the country, which they weren't. She ended up taking over the meeting and myself, Tom and Gordon, and a few others who were with us at the time, walked out. We didn't want any part of it. That was the creation of the Patriot Party. If you remember back then, there was a national movement called the Patriot Party. It didn't survive very long.

I went back to New York with Tom and Gordon, and we talked about starting a party in New York. Well that was George Pataki's first run for Governor of New York, and he was in a primary with a guy named Dick Rosenbaum. Dick was also from Rochester and he was the former Republican State Chairman. Tom, Gordon and myself asked Dick if he would be on the petition for us to start the party in 1994 and he agreed. So I went out, and using my experience from my run for Town Supervisor, I ran the petition drive. At that time nobody had ever done an independent petition drive in the state. I don't even know how I did it. I had six great people working with me. Bill Nield, my brother Charlie, David Stockmeister and others, and we literally traveled across the State of New York. We had to get a minimum of fifteen thousand signatures and we went from area to area to collect them. At that time there was also a group in New York City called the Fusion Party. That was a party that a couple of other mayors had run on unsuccessfully. I can't remember who ran it but Dick Morris was involved. They agreed to do the petitioning for us in the City of New York and then we hired another group to do the petitioning on Long Island.

Frank MacKay - So you never hired Lenora Fulani's group to do the petitioning in New York City?

Laureen Oliver: No, but the Fulanis saw that Tom Golisano had money, and that we were funding a state petition drive. At the time, she happened to be working for an organization in New York City that paid her to help them and they asked her to handle eleven districts for us in the City. She got involved because they paid her and that was my first sighting of Lenora Fulani. I'll never forget it. We went into a meeting, and I had read all about her before she walked into the meeting. I was not a happy camper. She was very nice to me, and Cathy Stewart was with her. I remember Gordon Black saying to me "be nice to her Laureen," and I said "no, this woman is not good news." I remember saying to her, "I don't care if you want to help or not, you have baggage and I have no baggage, and I have no intentions of carrying your baggage across the State of New York when we are trying to start a new party."

Fulani was getting involved with them and I was against it. Tom Golisano was against it too for the record. Gordon Black was the only friendlier one. You know, when we were doing the petition drive, there was only a handful of us, when the petition drive was over in June, and this group in NYC gave us their petitions, I will never forget it, I was in my brother's restaurant in Rochester, and we were cleaning up the petitions. Nothing illegal, but back them you had to put the Wards in, and if the Wards weren't there or certain things weren't on the petitions, the whole sheet would get thrown out. So we were checking the petitions, and the New York City organization delivered their signatures to us. They were worth toilet paper when I got them. They were so incomplete and I refused to pay them. I spoke with Tom Golisano and he said to pay them what I felt they were worth. I paid them half of the amount we originally agreed to.

Frank MacKay: Okay, so fast forward, what was the outcome of the election?

Laureen Oliver: Remember, Dick Rosenbaum was the candidate at that time and the Republicans and the Democrats left us alone. In September, the night of the Primary, Dick Rosenbaum lost the primary to George Pataki. At that time, there was a Republican County Executive in Rochester, and they all got together and they convinced Dick Rosenbaum to get off the petition. He agreed to get off and stabbed us in the back after we did all that work. He apologized, but needless to say, he got off the petition and we had 72 hours to fill the spot.

Frank MacKay: Did it take much convincing to get Tom Golisano to fill the vacancy?

Laureen Oliver: Tom was very supportive of the independent movement but he didn't want to run for Governor. His mother had recently passed away, and he was still the CEO and President of his company, Paychex, and very busy. I'll never forget it. So for 71 hours and 30 minutes, we waited for Tom to make his decision, and so finally he met us at the Post Office 30 minutes before the paperwork had to be signed and mailed, and agreed to run for Governor. Mind you, there were only six weeks left before the election.

Frank MacKay: And Tom Golisano was a big name too. He was a very rich guy, and still is, and he was also very passionate about political reform. Unlike Dick Rosenbaum, Golisano had to be considered a serious threat to the establishment.

Laureen Oliver: The minute Tom Golisano said yes, every big wig in the State of New York started taking pot shots at us. They started with trying to throw him off the ballot. Now let me explain the election law at that time. The right of substitution was only the right of the major parties and the major parties began taking us to court to prevent Tom from running. But Tom's position was, we were going to start spending money immediately. He started advertising. He spent somewhere around $8 million. I went on the ballot as the Comptroller.

Frank MacKay: You have to be very thick skinned to get past the lawsuits. That would make a lot of people uneasy, but it's a part of the battle when you are breaking ground in third party politics.

Laureen Oliver: We were being sued in every court in the State of New York over the substitution issue. We eventually won thanks to a Republican judge who also happened to be at odds with the local Republican Party.

Frank MacKay: That's a whole discussion in itself.

Laureen Oliver: Yes, but I have to tell you, the groundswell of support that came out for that five or six week campaign was tremendous. We had 250 volunteers working on the campaign and it was independent politics at its best. No one got paid. Golisano was out talking about what we stood for, because back then, people in other parties complained we didn't stand for anything.

Frank MacKay: They did it back then, and partisans in the New York print media and the major parties use that same mantra today too. Whenever there is a threat to their power and control, they begin making statements like the Independence Party doesn't stand for anything. We are a candidate driven party even today.

Laureen Oliver: The independence party was not created to be a party of inclusion. At that time in politics, all the polling showed that 70% of all Americans considered themselves moderates. We were the center. We wanted people who were fiscally conservative and socially moderate. The Democrats were too liberal, the Republicans were too conservative. We wanted to be the centrists. When we were creating the party, I would say, no - if you are liberal, go join the Liberal Party, and if you were right to life, go join the Conservative or Right to Life Party. We were socially moderate. Tom ran in 1994 and got 16% of the vote which gave the party ballot status in New York. From 1994 we went from what they called a "fledgling" party to the fourth line on the New York State ballot, in between the Conservative Party and the Liberal Party, which is where I joked we should have been, somewhere right in the middle. We really changed the course of future elections in New York. That line meant a lot. At that point we had to make a choice whether to keep the party going or kill it. Tom offered to give me some money to open a state office and hire some staff to keep it going.

Frank MacKay: It's been a very successful run. It's amazing how the New York print media has been so critical of the party over the years by stating that the Independence Party stands for nothing. This was a labor of love for you and all involved.

Laureen Oliver: Yes, hundreds of people came out to help develop the Party's bylaws and mission statement. Then we had to create county committees across the State. I was elected State Chair and screened over a thousand candidates in that first year. It was really fun and exciting at that time. We were really strict. We screened out any candidate that had a single issue. That was our litmus test. If they were really strong on one issue, we ruled them out. We were socially moderate and we did not want strong fringe candidates on the line. Back then, as we grew the party, the cross-endorsements in each county had to be evenly split.

Frank MacKay: That has all changed. In my own county, in Suffolk, we have elected 20 Independence Party members to public office.

Laureen Oliver: That's impressive, Frank. But after we got ballot status, we had the job of creating a Party. During the very first year, we had agreed to call the party the Independence-Fusion Party. Back then, there were 8-10 states in the nation that allowed fusion. Fusion is the term that allows a party to cross-endorse candidates. We used the name the first year, and we found the people didn't like it and we dropped "Fusion" from the name. My first role was to get county committees together. I went across the state to form county committees. The first Chairman I brought on was Jack Essenberg.

Frank MacKay: Yes, Jack Essenberg became the Suffolk County Independence Party Chairman and then you brought in Tom Pecoraro from Buffalo, NY.

Laureen Oliver: I met Tommy from the United We Stand movement. He was reluctant at first but I threatened to install one of his enemies in the position, and he agreed to do it. I wanted him because he was a very strong organizer. Buffalo was one of the hardest counties to work with. I allowed the County chairs to pick their county committees and I did a lot of traveling throughout the state, just like you have done, to get them organized. I would bring the county chairs in every three months for meetings as well. I had wonderful county chairs, such as Jeff Graham from Watertown and Brian Kaiser from Syracuse. I was looking for people who would work the party and not be there simply to make names for themselves. By the time Jack Essenberg took over as Chair, I had installed county chairs in 47 of New York's 62 counties.

Frank MacKay: So if I recall, by this time, you were also working on the national front to build a third party in the country.

Laureen Oliver: 1996 was the presidential run and that was a funny year. Perot ran again. Gordon Black was Perot's pollster in 1994. So in 1996, when he decided he was going to run, United We Stand had fallen by the wayside in New York. Gordon Black and Tom Golisano had gone down to see Ross Perot and tried to convince him to start an independent political party during his run by taking United We Stand and converting it to a political party. Perot didn't want to do that. Tom and Gordon left the room and unbeknownst to Tom Golisano, Gordon went back into the room and told Ross Perot that if he didn't start a national political party with United We Stand, that Tom Golisano would do it. Golisano was a billionaire by that time, and Perot took it seriously. That's how the Reform Party came about.

Frank MacKay: We all know the fate of the Reform Party.

Laureen Oliver: Perot couldn't have a Reform Party without New York. The Independence Party was already an established party, but for the benefit of all the other independent organizations in the country, we joined the Reform Party back then. However, when they did their ballot for the Presidential candidates at the Reform Party convention in 1996, between Dick Lamm and Ross Perot, I gave the nominating speech for Lamm, along with Dean Barkley and Tom D'Amore. Tom was instrumental in independent politics even before me. He knew more about independent politics than anyone I know. Needless to say, Perot went on to get the Reform Party's nomination in 1996. The Independence Party of New York went on and we grew and became more influential. 1998 came around and I was still State Chair of the Party.

Frank MacKay: Then you decided to make another run at political office. Tell us about what made you decide to run for Lt. Governor of New York in 1998.

Laureen Oliver: Once again, Tom Golisano was going to run for Governor. He ran in 1994 to establish the party and in 1998, he ran to save the party. I was State Chair, and the State Committee was debating who was going to run for Lt. Governor. In the meeting, Jeff Graham wanted to run for Lt. Governor but the Fulanis wouldn't support him. That year, I became the compromise candidate and I ran for Lt. Governor as Tom' running mate. It was a great year. We became the third largest party in the State of New York.

Frank MacKay: Yes, and Jesse Ventura won election in Minnesota the same night.

Laureen Oliver: Yes, Jesse Ventura became Governor. On the national level we worked very closely with the Minnesota Party. In 1998, we became the tail that wagged the dog. In 1999, we

had more requests for candidate endorsements than the Democratic and Republican parties collectively. In 1999, I also started to think I needed a life. I had separated from my husband and I decided to step down. My decision to step down as Chair was for both personal and political reasons. In New York, the weighted vote is determined by what their gubernatorial candidate got in the last election. Because Tom Golisano was the candidate in 1998, Rochester and the surrounding counties carried more than 50% of the weighted vote in the election. I had a considerable amount of power in the State but I didn't want the Independence Party to turn into an upstate party.

Frank MacKay: That's pretty honorable of you. Most people would not think that way.

Laureen Oliver: I used to bitch all the time about what the State Chairs were doing in the other parties, such as Mike Long. I could have done what Mike Long was doing and perfected it if I wanted to. At that time I controlled the third line on the ballot. I use the word control because we did not have constituted county committees at the time. It was me and my committee who controlled who our county chairs were. We controlled it out of Rochester because we started the party. I didn't want it to stay that way.

Frank MacKay: I give you a lot of credit, Laureen, for all the work you did to launch the Independence Party in New York State. I know you moved to Florida, and Tom Golisano relocated as well, and you have both stayed very active in politics on the national front. Tell me about how and why you teamed up to change the Electoral College system in the United States.

Laureen Oliver: A few years ago, during dinner with Tom Golisano in Florida, I talked with him about this very issue. Tom is someone who wants to make a difference in this country, but he doesn't want to be a candidate. During this discussion, I suggested we work on how electors are awarded in presidential elections. Electors are awarded in the presidential election under the winner takes all system in the states, and there have been four debacles in which the populist candidate has not won.

I felt it was going to get worse as the number of independent voters increased and outnumbered the registered Democrats and Republicans in the country. Well needless to say, right after that meeting, we created Support Popular Vote and then we hooked up with an organization called National Popular Vote. That's the bill out there today -- it's called the National Popular Vote bill, which got passed in the State of New York recently. It's a combine bill, a bill between states. It says that on the night of the election, your electors, not the Electoral College, award your votes to the candidate that received the most votes in the country, versus the most votes in your state. Now, you don't even have to do the whole country. You only have to get half of the 540 to change the system.

Frank MacKay: I agree, this changes everything. This is a big deal.

Laureen Oliver: So if states that equal 270 electors join this bill, and we are probably close to 200 or more, then on election night, the candidate that wins the popular vote will be elected President of the United States. So Tom and I worked on this issue for a few years and Tom spent a lot of money on it.

Frank MacKay: I'm thrilled that Governor Cuomo signed this bill into law in April 2014. I really hope that other states follow suit. If we reach 270 electors, it will be one of the most significant political reforms in our nation's history, and I know we'll have Tom Golisano to thank for the effort and money he has put into educating people on this piece of legislation. It is very significant and could open the floodgates for fair elections. That's really Tom's style in a lot of ways. He works behind the scenes on significant political reform laws. Has Tom talked recently about coming back into the spotlight and possibly running for President as an independent?

Laureen Oliver: In 2012, there was a group courting Tom Golisano for President. He is, in my eyes, the candidate we should have had for President. Tom Golisano can't be bought, and more importantly, he doesn't look at bills and laws from the eyes of the two-party system. He looks at bills and what we should do based on their merit. He would have been the one candidate for President that would have brought this country together. In 2012, there was one night when he came close to saying yes. He would have been on every ballot in the nation, and he screened candidates for Vice President. It was very serious, but Tom has worked a long time in his life, and he got to the stage where felt he didn't want to do it. I think till this day he thinks about it and I think he would have been a great President. He ran three times for Governor and three 3 times he told the voters of New York the problems that were coming; not balancing the budget, the back door borrowing, the interest rates, all the things he stood for. Everything he said came true.

Frank MacKay: Do you think an independent could win a race for the presidency?

Laureen Oliver: Back then in the early 90s, about 20% of the voters in the country were registered independent, and today in a lot of states, independents are outnumbering the Democrats and Republicans. If you've ever looked at a chart of registered voters you will see the bulk of registered Republicans are seniors. The Democratic line doesn't have the same age angle; it is a relative stable pool of voters across age groups. Democrats have more special interest groups, such as unions, and the age demographics are blended. Independents go the opposite way. It starts out with the bulk of its voters as younger people and decreases as people get older. As the baby boomers become seniors, the independents become the larger pool and the Republicans decrease with time. The day will come that the Republican Party is gone. Unless they figure out how to get young voters and minorities into their party, they can't survive.

Frank MacKay: The door is opening for an independent to run and win. I want to thank you for coming on the show, Laureen. It's been great talking with you.

Laureen Oliver: Thanks, Frank. It was great talking with you too.

I was elected in the year 2000 with the support of Stewart and Laureen Oliver. As State Chair, I have supported a "local autonomy" configuration that has given grassroots activists the power to choose and endorse candidates for elective office that best suited the values and objectives of their area of jurisdiction.

An Independent for President

The Independence Party of New York has sculpted its umbrella platform to attract the greatest number of participants by avoiding the inclusion of polarizing and divisive social issues in its mission. This political model may well offer the greatest opportunity for change to take place in the wide spectrum of the American electorate and provide a viable third choice at the polls.

The Independence Party of America promises to bring independents and non-voters together into an organized and powerful voting bloc by giving more power to the people. It will shun the partisan alliances that lead to stagnation in government, and cultivate leadership that will be less reliant on heavily financed special interests. As unbelievable as this may appear on the surface, America has cultivated possibly thousands of people who may meet this new political leadership prototype: the pool of people we are considering are comprised of nation's successful entrepreneurs who have made their money in the private sector, learned through experience how to manage people and complicated systems, and who have a special personal interest in the great challenge of fixing a system that is suffering from decades of mismanagement and runaway federal spending.

The ideal independent candidates will have a unique interest in creating opportunities for others to follow in their path to success, and be willing to deconstruct the bureaucracy and rebuild it upon a strong foundation. They will be mindful of the roadblocks to achieving the American dreams of homeownership, a good education and quality health care, and be creative in finding solutions to repairing the nation's crumbling infrastructure. They will also be highly adept at foreign affairs, with excellent communication skills to help put America — and the world --on the right course to achieving lasting peace.

The Independence Party of America was created as a mechanism for independents to launch a non-partisan presidential candidate, but it will take a national effort of independent organizations across the country, and an army of dedicated volunteers. It will also take an army of savvy political operatives in each state to make it a reality.

Independent activists could carry on forever being utilized by the major parties, or instead, meld into a collective body politic that could rival the major parties, and elect an independent President. If independent third party political operatives throughout the nation could pull together, state by state, through an organized mechanism of *local autonomy*, there would be a very good chance that there would be organization in place to cultivate a new prototype of a politician who would represent the collective spirit of our citizenry – not Democrat or Republican, but an American Independent.

Political operatives may have an unsavory reputation in the United States, and quite frankly, they are highly distrusted because as their name implies, they are "operators". However, many Americans fail to realize that it is the operatives that play a key role in choosing candidates that appear on ballots – from the village clerk to President, and it begins with the political organizations and the people who make up those organizations. For better or worse, the Party systems – and the people that make up the structure of those systems -- vet nearly all candidates running for public office. Most voters could not name even the local leaders of their major party political organizations, or even the national leadership, but they have a tremendous influence on the shifting priorities of the nation, the choice of candidates who run for public office and the candidates' platforms. Political party leaders are essential to rallying up votes for their candidates and motivating volunteers.

It is important that as we build a new independent movement that political leaders understand their role. Our strategy should be to set up an infrastructure to achieve ballot access and rally volunteers, but that is where is should end. If we truly want to set up a vehicle to allow a political independent to do his or her job for the American people, it's critically important that political leaders stay out of the business of influencing candidates' political platforms and the business of governing.

Nonetheless, political party structures are built on volunteers and savvy political operatives that guide campaigns, assess public opinion and manage their candidates' schedules. Some of the most well-known political operatives in the nation are Karl Rove (R), Dick Morris (D), James Carville (D), Mary Matalin (R), Ed Rollins (R) and the late Hamilton Jordan (D) and Lee Atwater (R). In New York State, Thomas Connolly, Vice Chair of the Independence Party of New York, is one of the most brilliant political strategists in the business. He is my right hand in the State party, and is a major part of the success of the third party movement over the years.

While most operatives work behind the scenes, the media has taken a special interest in these individuals and their work. Their jobs are to win elections. Period. And for an independent non-major party candidate to win the presidency, the Independence Party of America will need them too. However, if we are going to change the way politics is done in the United States, and truly regain the faith of the People, we are going to do it differently. There is a way, and there is certainly public interest.

There are literally millions of independents without a home base, and perhaps some trepidation about aligning themselves with another political party. Thus, the glue that will bind independents into a powerful voting bloc will be the men and women who work for a common goal, and the independent candidate who rises from the grassroots.

The Independent movement needs spokespeople and savvy political operatives; people who love the game and have a sincere interest in changing the direction of the country. We need successful, smart and active citizens who are tired of the status quo and want to help build a party around a candidate. In every county, in every city throughout the nation, from villages to state capitals, there are people with a political conscience that are motivated to change the system. Simply said, they need to step up to the plate. Whatever the motive may be to become a reformer, their reward will be a place in history during the infancy of a transformation in American politics.

Our success will depend on who shows up to work.

From "Spoiling" to Winning

It is often claimed that the American electoral system is "set up" to prevent a third party candidate from winning a national election. Can an independent candidate make the jump from so-called spoiler to winner?

To answer this question, and discuss the role of political operatives, I spoke with Thomas Connolly, Vice Chair of the Independence Party of New York.

Polls done throughout the last decade consistently report that more than sixty percent of Americans favor a strong third major party that would run candidates for president, congress, and state offices. Nearly a third of Americans consider themselves independents, which has been demonstrated in recent years by the high level of vote splitting among the American electorate.

Clearly the tide is turning in favor of an independent bid for the presidency. The door to the White House is slowly opening for the American Independent. The right candidate can open the floodgates.

Even so, when it comes down to math, winning won't be easy for a third party candidate. There are a total of 538 electoral votes up for grabs among the 50 states. The candidate who wins enough states to reach 270 electoral votes wins the presidency. If all candidates fall under the required electoral votes, the president-elect would be selected by a vote of the House of Representatives. Each House Member is given one vote in this case. If no vice presidential candidate receives a majority, then the vice president-elect is selected by a vote of the Senate. This scenario has not occurred since 1825 and 1837.

The bottom line for an independent candidate is to capture 270 electoral votes. A qualified non-partisan candidate with sufficient name recognition could arguably achieve the required votes, but it would have to be the right person. Leadership qualities, intellectual, financial, political acumen, and clearly a strong ethical character, must be benchmarks for reform-minded operatives in their efforts to draft an ideal independent candidate for a presidential race. We must work to ensure the public trust follows as we embark on this mission to find our next president; or we will fail.

A presidential candidate also needs to receive the highest numbers of votes in the right combination of states to win a majority of the electoral vote to win the race. A candidate may in fact win the popular vote, but it is electoral votes that count, literally.

In the case of the 2000 election, Al Gore received the popular vote, and George Bush became president because he won a plurality of votes in Florida with the help of third party candidate Ralph Nader, who acted as a vote-peeler. After a highly disputed vote recount all of Florida's electoral votes went to George Bush.

This lesson in American history drove home two major points: it is time for Congress to scrap the Electoral College for a popular vote system or award electoral votes in proportion to the candidates' share of the vote in each state. In the meantime, in order to be elected President of the United States, the major parties tend to focus the majority of their time and money on winning key "battleground" states. However, if you are not a major party candidate, you need to run an effective ground war in all fifty states.

In order to do this, the ideal candidate must have the power – of the celebrity-status caliber – to reach beyond the activists and draw previous non-voters and infrequent voters into the American electorate.

These groups will form the natural basis for the candidate's ballot access campaign in each of the fifty states and the District of Columbia. While it will not be necessary to be on the ballot in all fifty states to win the White House, from a psychological standpoint, Americans from coast to coast must have the ability to cast their vote for the non-major party candidate, or the election's outcome could be highly unpopular.

Ballot access is one of those complicated concepts that even seasoned social and political activists have difficulty understanding. Simply put, each state has its own unique ballot access laws and these laws provide the 'rules' by which individuals must conform to have their name appear in the voting booth or ballots on Election Day. Some states have relatively simple rules to follow, but most make it very complicated to run for public office. This precludes many average citizens from making the jump from activist to candidate, and it is a shame. It also creates high paying jobs for election lawyers and political consultants!

Republicans or Democrats need to collect a minimum of 23,500 valid signatures to appear on the ballot in all fifty states, but a new party needs to collect a minimum of 625,000 valid signatures to achieve ballot access for their candidate. An independent candidate could run on an existing Party line, such as the Independence Party of New York, or they could petition in each state to create a new political party, or temporary 'line' on the ballot.

Achieving ballot access requires the work of thousands of volunteers and paid workers nationwide, and it is a difficult task for the average third party hopeful. A summary of state ballot access laws, prepared by the National Association of

Secretaries of State and reprinted with their permission, is included in the following pages.

The right candidate must be able to motivate and mobilize the nation's volunteers to achieve ballot status in each state. The bottom line is that electing a non-major party candidate for the presidency will require hard work and mass mobilization, but most importantly it will require the right candidate for our times. In the words of Martin Luther King, Jr: *"A genuine leader is not a searcher for consensus but a molder of consensus."*[3]

The right candidate will also need a blueprint for a fifty state ballot access plan. The National Association of the Secretaries of State published a guide to the state laws in the year 2012, and with their permission, I have included a reprint of their guide in the appendix. Keep in mind that these guidelines refer to the last presidential election cycle, and in some cases, it cites specific deadlines that would no longer be relevant. In these cases, I have placed brackets around the dates. These laws and specific dates are subject to change. It is important to note that I decided to include this information as an educational reference about the ballot access laws in all fifty states, but anyone interested in embarking on a presidential election or political party ballot access plan must check current laws with their local election boards and the Secretary of State in the jurisdiction.

If you would like to join the Independence movement, visit us online at: www.independencepartyny.com.

If this book inspires one person to pursue a candidacy for President as an independent, we have done a great service to the country. A third major party will only be possible with the right candidate stepping forward.

---

[3] (Speech: Domestic Impact of War, November 1967)

GEORGE WASHINGTON'S FAREWELL ADDRESS

FRIENDS AND FELLOW-CITIZENS:

1 The period for a new election of a citizen, to administer the executive government of the United States, being not far distant, and the time actually arrived, when your thoughts must be employed designating the person, who is to be clothed with that important trust, it appears to me proper, especially as it may conduce to a more distinct expression of the public voice, that I should now apprize you of the resolution I have formed, to decline being considered among the number of those out of whom a choice is to be made.

2 I beg you at the same time to do me the justice to be assured that this resolution has not been taken without a strict regard to all the considerations appertaining to the relation which binds a dutiful citizen to his country; and that in withdrawing the tender of service, which silence in my situation might imply, I am influenced by no diminution of zeal for your future interest, no deficiency of grateful respect for your past kindness, but am supported by a full conviction that the step is compatible with both.

3 The acceptance of, and continuance hitherto in, the office to which your suffrages have twice called me, have been a uniform sacrifice of inclination to the opinion of duty, and to a deference for what appeared to be your desire. I constantly hoped, that it would have been much

earlier in my power, consistently with motives, which I was not at liberty to disregard, to return to that retirement, from which I had been reluctantly drawn. The strength of my inclination to do this, previous to the last election, had even led to the preparation of an address to declare it to you; but mature reflection on the then perplexed and critical posture of our affairs with foreign nations, and the unanimous advice of persons entitled to my confidence impelled me to abandon the idea.

4 I rejoice, that the state of your concerns, external as well as internal, no longer renders the pursuit of inclination incompatible with the sentiment of duty, or propriety; and am persuaded, whatever partiality may be retained for my services, that, in the present circumstances of our country, you will not disapprove my determination to retire.

5 The impressions, with which I first undertook the arduous trust, were explained on the proper occasion. In the discharge of this trust, I will only say, that I have, with good intentions, contributed towards the organization and administration of the government the best exertions of which a very fallible judgment was capable. Not unconscious, in the outset, of the inferiority of my qualifications, experience in my own eyes, perhaps still more in the eyes of others, has strengthened the motives to diffidence of myself; and every day the increasing weight of years admonishes me more and more, that the shade of retirement is as necessary to me as it will be welcome. Satisfied, that, if any circumstances have given peculiar value to my services, they were temporary, I have the consolation to believe, that, while choice and

prudence invite me to quit the political scene, patriotism does not forbid it.

6 In looking forward to the moment, which is intended to terminate the career of my public life, my feelings do not permit me to suspend the deep acknowledgment of that debt of gratitude, which I owe to my beloved country for the many honors it has conferred upon me; still more for the steadfast confidence with which it has supported me; and for the opportunities I have thence enjoyed of manifesting my inviolable attachment, by services faithful and persevering, though in usefulness unequal to my zeal. If benefits have resulted to our country from these services, let it always be remembered to your praise, and as an instructive example in our annals, that under circumstances in which the passions, agitated in every direction, were liable to mislead, amidst appearances sometimes dubious, vicissitudes of fortune often discouraging, in situations in which not unfrequently want of success has countenanced the spirit of criticism, the constancy of your support was the essential prop of the efforts, and a guarantee of the plans by which they were effected. Profoundly penetrated with this idea, I shall carry it with me to my grave, as a strong incitement to unceasing vows that Heaven may continue to you the choicest tokens of its beneficence; that your union and brotherly affection may be perpetual; that the free constitution, which is the work of your hands, may be sacredly maintained; that its administration in every department may be stamped with wisdom and virtue; than, in fine, the happiness of the people of these States, under the auspices of liberty, may be made

complete, by so careful a preservation and so prudent a use of this blessing, as will acquire to them the glory of recommending it to the applause, the affection, and adoption of every nation, which is yet a stranger to it.

7 Here, perhaps I ought to stop. But a solicitude for your welfare which cannot end but with my life, and the apprehension of danger, natural to that solicitude, urge me, on an occasion like the present, to offer to your solemn contemplation, and to recommend to your frequent review, some sentiments which are the result of much reflection, of no inconsiderable observation, and which appear to me all-important to the permanency of your felicity as a people. These will be offered to you with the more freedom, as you can only see in them the disinterested warnings of a parting friend, who can possibly have no personal motive to bias his counsel. Nor can I forget, as an encouragement to it, your indulgent reception of my sentiments on a former and not dissimilar occasion.

8 Interwoven as is the love of liberty with every ligament of your hearts, no recommendation of mine is necessary to fortify or confirm the attachment.

9 The unity of Government, which constitutes you one people, is also now dear to you. It is justly so; for it is a main pillar in the edifice of your real independence, the support of your tranquillity at home, your peace abroad; of your safety; of your prosperity; of that very Liberty, which you so highly prize. But as it is easy to foresee, that, from

different causes and from different quarters, much pains will be taken, many artifices employed, to weaken in your minds the conviction of this truth; as this is the point in your political fortress against which the batteries of internal and external enemies will be most constantly and actively (though often covertly and insidiously) directed, it is of infinite moment, that you should properly estimate the immense value of your national Union to your collective and individual happiness; that you should cherish a cordial, habitual, and immovable attachment to it; accustoming yourselves to think and speak of it as of the Palladium of your political safety and prosperity; watching for its preservation with jealous anxiety; discountenancing whatever may suggest even a suspicion, that it can in any event be abandoned; and indignantly frowning upon the first dawning of every attempt to alienate any portion of our country from the rest, or to enfeeble the sacred ties which now link together the various parts.

10 For this you have every inducement of sympathy and interest. Citizens, by birth or choice, of a common country, that country has a right to concentrate your affections. The name of american, which belongs to you, in your national capacity, must always exalt the just pride of Patriotism, more than any appellation derived from local discriminations. With slight shades of difference, you have the same religion, manners, habits, and political principles. You have in a common cause fought and triumphed together; the Independence and Liberty you possess are the work of joint counsels, and joint efforts, of common dangers, sufferings, and successes.

11 But these considerations, however powerfully they address themselves to your sensibility, are greatly outweighed by those, which apply more immediately to your interest. Here every portion of our country finds the most commanding motives for carefully guarding and preserving the Union of the whole.

12 The North, in an unrestrained intercourse with the South, protected by the equal laws of a common government, finds, in the productions of the latter, great additional resources of maritime and commercial enterprise and precious materials of manufacturing industry. The South, in the same intercourse, benefiting by the agency of the North, sees its agriculture grow and its commerce expand. Turning partly into its own channels the seamen of the North, it finds its particular navigation invigorated; and, while it contributes, in different ways, to nourish and increase the general mass of the national navigation, it looks forward to the protection of a maritime strength, to which itself is unequally adapted. The East, in a like intercourse with the West, already finds, and in the progressive improvement of interior communications by land and water, will more and more find, a valuable vent for the commodities which it brings from abroad, or manufactures at home. The West derives from the East supplies requisite to its growth and comfort, and, what is perhaps of still greater consequence, it must of necessity owe the secure enjoyment of indispensable outlets for its own productions to the weight, influence, and the future maritime strength of the Atlantic side of the Union, directed by an indissoluble community of interest as one nation. Any

other tenure by which the West can hold this essential advantage, whether derived from its own separate strength, or from an apostate and unnatural connexion with any foreign power, must be intrinsically precarious.

13 While, then, every part of our country thus feels an immediate and particular interest in Union, all the parts combined cannot fail to find in the united mass of means and efforts greater strength, greater resource, proportionably greater security from external danger, a less frequent interruption of their peace by foreign nations; and, what is of inestimable value, they must derive from Union an exemption from those broils and wars between themselves, which so frequently afflict neighbouring countries not tied together by the same governments, which their own rivalships alone would be sufficient to produce, but which opposite foreign alliances, attachments, and intrigues would stimulate and embitter. Hence, likewise, they will avoid the necessity of those overgrown military establishments, which, under any form of government, are inauspicious to liberty, and which are to be regarded as particularly hostile to Republican Liberty. In this sense it is, that your Union ought to be considered as a main prop of your liberty, and that the love of the one ought to endear to you the preservation of the other.

14 These considerations speak a persuasive language to every reflecting and virtuous mind, and exhibit the continuance of the union as a primary object of Patriotic desire. Is there a doubt, whether a common government can embrace so large a sphere? Let experience

solve it. To listen to mere speculation in such a case were criminal. We are authorized to hope, that a proper organization of the whole, with the auxiliary agency of governments for the respective subdivisions, will afford a happy issue to the experiment. It is well worth a fair and full experiment. With such powerful and obvious motives to Union, affecting all parts of our country, while experience shall not have demonstrated its impracticability, there will always be reason to distrust the patriotism of those, who in any quarter may endeavour to weaken its bands.

15 In contemplating the causes, which may disturb our Union, it occurs as matter of serious concern, that any ground should have been furnished for characterizing parties by Geographical discriminations, Northern and Southern, Atlantic and Western; whence designing men may endeavour to excite a belief, that there is a real difference of local interests and views. One of the expedients of party to acquire influence, within particular districts, is to misrepresent the opinions and aims of other districts. You cannot shield yourselves too much against the jealousies and heart-burnings, which spring from these misrepresentations; they tend to render alien to each other those, who ought to be bound together by fraternal affection. The inhabitants of our western country have lately had a useful lesson on this head; they have seen, in the negotiation by the Executive, and in the unanimous ratification by the Senate, of the treaty with Spain, and in the universal satisfaction at that event, throughout the United States, a decisive proof how unfounded were the suspicions propagated among them of a

policy in the General Government and in the Atlantic States unfriendly to their interests in regard to the mississippi; they have been witnesses to the formation of two treaties, that with Great Britain, and that with Spain, which secure to them every thing they could desire, in respect to our foreign relations, towards confirming their prosperity. Will it not be their wisdom to rely for the preservation of these advantages on the union by which they were procured? Will they not henceforth be deaf to those advisers, if such there are, who would sever them from their brethren, and connect them with aliens?

16 To the efficacy and permanency of your Union, a Government for the whole is indispensable. No alliances, however strict, between the parts can be an adequate substitute; they must inevitably experience the infractions and interruptions, which all alliances in all times have experienced. Sensible of this momentous truth, you have improved upon your first essay, by the adoption of a Constitution of Government better calculated than your former for an intimate Union, and for the efficacious management of your common concerns. This Government, the offspring of our own choice, uninfluenced and unawed, adopted upon full investigation and mature deliberation, completely free in its principles, in the distribution of its powers, uniting security with energy, and containing within itself a provision for its own amendment, has a just claim to your confidence and your support. Respect for its authority, compliance with its laws, acquiescence in its measures, are duties enjoined by the fundamental maxims of true Liberty. The basis of our political systems is the right of the people to

make and to alter their Constitutions of Government. But the Constitution which at any time exists, till changed by an explicit and authentic act of the whole people, is sacredly obligatory upon all. The very idea of the power and the right of the people to establish Government presupposes the duty of every individual to obey the established Government.

17 All obstructions to the execution of the Laws, all combinations and associations, under whatever plausible character, with the real design to direct, control, counteract, or awe the regular deliberation and action of the constituted authorities, are destructive of this fundamental principle, and of fatal tendency. They serve to organize faction, to give it an artificial and extraordinary force; to put, in the place of the delegated will of the nation, the will of a party, often a small but artful and enterprising minority of the community; and, according to the alternate triumphs of different parties, to make the public administration the mirror of the ill-concerted and incongruous projects of faction, rather than the organ of consistent and wholesome plans digested by common counsels, and modified by mutual interests.

18 However combinations or associations of the above description may now and then answer popular ends, they are likely, in the course of time and things, to become potent engines, by which cunning, ambitious, and unprincipled men will be enabled to subvert the power of the people, and to usurp for themselves the reins of government; destroying afterwards the very engines, which have lifted them to unjust dominion.

19 Towards the preservation of your government, and the permanency of your present happy state, it is requisite, not only that you steadily discountenance irregular oppositions to its acknowledged authority, but also that you resist with care the spirit of innovation upon its principles, however specious the pretexts. One method of assault may be to effect, in the forms of the constitution, alterations, which will impair the energy of the system, and thus to undermine what cannot be directly overthrown. In all the changes to which you may be invited, remember that time and habit are at least as necessary to fix the true character of governments, as of other human institutions; that experience is the surest standard, by which to test the real tendency of the existing constitution of a country; that facility in changes, upon the credit of mere hypothesis and opinion, exposes to perpetual change, from the endless variety of hypothesis and opinion; and remember, especially, that, for the efficient management of our common interests, in a country so extensive as ours, a government of as much vigor as is consistent with the perfect security of liberty is indispensable. Liberty itself will find in such a government, with powers properly distributed and adjusted, its surest guardian. It is, indeed, little else than a name, where the government is too feeble to withstand the enterprises of faction, to confine each member of the society within the limits prescribed by the laws, and to maintain all in the secure and tranquil enjoyment of the rights of person and property.

20 I have already intimated to you the danger of parties in the state, with particular reference to the founding of them on geographical

discriminations. Let me now take a more comprehensive view, and warn you in the most solemn manner against the baneful effects of the spirit of party, generally.

21 This spirit, unfortunately, is inseparable from our nature, having its root in the strongest passions of the human mind. It exists under different shapes in all governments, more or less stifled, controlled, or repressed; but, in those of the popular form, it is seen in its greatest rankness, and is truly their worst enemy.

22 The alternate domination of one faction over another, sharpened by the spirit of revenge, natural to party dissension, which in different ages and countries has perpetrated the most horrid enormities, is itself a frightful despotism. But this leads at length to a more formal and permanent despotism. The disorders and miseries, which result, gradually incline the minds of men to seek security and repose in the absolute power of an individual; and sooner or later the chief of some prevailing faction, more able or more fortunate than his competitors, turns this disposition to the purposes of his own elevation, on the ruins of Public Liberty.

23 Without looking forward to an extremity of this kind, (which nevertheless ought not to be entirely out of sight,) the common and continual mischiefs of the spirit of party are sufficient to make it the interest and duty of a wise people to discourage and restrain it.

24 It serves always to distract the Public Councils, and enfeeble the Public Administration. It agitates the Community with ill-founded jealousies and false alarms; kindles the animosity of one part against another, foments occasionally riot and insurrection. It opens the door to foreign influence and corruption, which find a facilitated access to the government itself through the channels of party passions. Thus the policy and the will of one country are subjected to the policy and will of another.

25 There is an opinion, that parties in free countries are useful checks upon the administration of the Government, and serve to keep alive the spirit of Liberty. This within certain limits is probably true; and in Governments of a Monarchical cast, Patriotism may look with indulgence, if not with favor, upon the spirit of party. But in those of the popular character, in Governments purely elective, it is a spirit not to be encouraged. From their natural tendency, it is certain there will always be enough of that spirit for every salutary purpose. And, there being constant danger of excess, the effort ought to be, by force of public opinion, to mitigate and assuage it. A fire not to be quenched, it demands a uniform vigilance to prevent its bursting into a flame, lest, instead of warming, it should consume.

26 It is important, likewise, that the habits of thinking in a free country should inspire caution, in those intrusted with its administration, to confine themselves within their respective constitutional spheres, avoiding in the exercise of the powers of one department to encroach upon another. The spirit of encroachment tends to consolidate the

powers of all the departments in one, and thus to create, whatever the form of government, a real despotism. A just estimate of that love of power, and proneness to abuse it, which predominates in the human heart, is sufficient to satisfy us of the truth of this position. The necessity of reciprocal checks in the exercise of political power, by dividing and distributing it into different depositories, and constituting each the Guardian of the Public Weal against invasions by the others, has been evinced by experiments ancient and modern; some of them in our country and under our own eyes. To preserve them must be as necessary as to institute them. If, in the opinion of the people, the distribution or modification of the constitutional powers be in any particular wrong, let it be corrected by an amendment in the way, which the constitution designates. But let there be no change by usurpation; for, though this, in one instance, may be the instrument of good, it is the customary weapon by which free governments are destroyed. The precedent must always greatly overbalance in permanent evil any partial or transient benefit, which the use can at any time yield.

27 Of all the dispositions and habits, which lead to political prosperity, Religion and Morality are indispensable supports. In vain would that man claim the tribute of Patriotism, who should labor to subvert these great pillars of human happiness, these firmest props of the duties of Men and Citizens. The mere Politician, equally with the pious man, ought to respect and to cherish them. A volume could not trace all their connexions with private and public felicity. Let it simply be asked,

Where is the security for property, for reputation, for life, if the sense of religious obligation desert the oaths, which are the instruments of investigation in Courts of Justice? And let us with caution indulge the supposition, that morality can be maintained without religion. Whatever may be conceded to the influence of refined education on minds of peculiar structure, reason and experience both forbid us to expect, that national morality can prevail in exclusion of religious principle.

28 It is substantially true, that virtue or morality is a necessary spring of popular government. The rule, indeed, extends with more or less force to every species of free government. Who, that is a sincere friend to it, can look with indifference upon attempts to shake the foundation of the fabric ?

29 Promote, then, as an object of primary importance, institutions for the general diffusion of knowledge. In proportion as the structure of a government gives force to public opinion, it is essential that public opinion should be enlightened.

30 As a very important source of strength and security, cherish public credit. One method of preserving it is, to use it as sparingly as possible; avoiding occasions of expense by cultivating peace, but remembering also that timely disbursements to prepare for danger frequently prevent much greater disbursements to repel it; avoiding likewise the accumulation of debt, not only by shunning occasions of expense, but by vigorous exertions in time of peace to discharge the

debts, which unavoidable wars may have occasioned, not ungenerously throwing upon posterity the burthen, which we ourselves ought to bear. The execution of these maxims belongs to your representatives, but it is necessary that public opinion should cooperate. To facilitate to them the performance of their duty, it is essential that you should practically bear in mind, that towards the payment of debts there must be Revenue; that to have Revenue there must be taxes; that no taxes can be devised, which are not more or less inconvenient and unpleasant; that the intrinsic embarrassment, inseparable from the selection of the proper objects (which is always a choice of difficulties), ought to be a decisive motive for a candid construction of the conduct of the government in making it, and for a spirit of acquiescence in the measures for obtaining revenue, which the public exigencies may at any time dictate.

31 Observe good faith and justice towards all Nations; cultivate peace and harmony with all. Religion and Morality enjoin this conduct; and can it be, that good policy does not equally enjoin it? It will be worthy of a free, enlightened, and, at no distant period, a great Nation, to give to mankind the magnanimous and too novel example of a people always guided by an exalted justice and benevolence. Who can doubt, that, in the course of time and things, the fruits of such a plan would richly repay any temporary advantages, which might be lost by a steady adherence to it ? Can it be, that Providence has not connected the permanent felicity of a Nation with its Virtue? The experiment, at

least, is recommended by every sentiment which ennobles human nature. Alas! is it rendered impossible by its vices ?

32 In the execution of such a plan, nothing is more essential, than that permanent, inveterate antipathies against particular Nations, and passionate attachments for others, should be excluded; and that, in place of them, just and amicable feelings towards all should be cultivated. The Nation, which indulges towards another an habitual hatred, or an habitual fondness, is in some degree a slave. It is a slave to its animosity or to its affection, either of which is sufficient to lead it astray from its duty and its interest. Antipathy in one nation against another disposes each more readily to offer insult and injury, to lay hold of slight causes of umbrage, and to be haughty and intractable, when accidental or trifling occasions of dispute occur. Hence frequent collisions, obstinate, envenomed, and bloody contests. The Nation, prompted by ill-will and resentment, sometimes impels to war the Government, contrary to the best calculations of policy. The Government sometimes participates in the national propensity, and adopts through passion what reason would reject; at other times, it makes the animosity of the nation subservient to projects of hostility instigated by pride, ambition, and other sinister and pernicious motives. The peace often, sometimes perhaps the liberty, of Nations has been the victim.

33 So likewise, a passionate attachment of one Nation for another produces a variety of evils. Sympathy for the favorite Nation, facilitating the illusion of an imaginary common interest, in cases

where no real common interest exists, and infusing into one the
enmities of the other, betrays the former into a participation in the
quarrels and wars of the latter, without adequate inducement or
justification. It leads also to concessions to the favorite Nation of
privileges denied to others, which is apt doubly to injure the Nation
making the concessions; by unnecessarily parting with what ought to
have been retained; and by exciting jealousy, ill-will, and a disposition
to retaliate, in the parties from whom equal privileges are withheld.
And it gives to ambitious, corrupted, or deluded citizens, (who devote
themselves to the favorite nation,) facility to betray or sacrifice the
interests of their own country, without odium, sometimes even with
popularity; gilding, with the appearances of a virtuous sense of
obligation, a commendable deference for public opinion, or a laudable
zeal for public good, the base or foolish compliances of ambition,
corruption, or infatuation.

34 As avenues to foreign influence in innumerable ways, such
attachments are particularly alarming to the truly enlightened and
independent Patriot. How many opportunities do they afford to tamper
with domestic factions, to practise the arts of seduction, to mislead
public opinion, to influence or awe the Public Councils! Such an
attachment of a small or weak, towards a great and powerful nation,
dooms the former to be the satellite of the latter.

35 Against the insidious wiles of foreign influence (I conjure you to
believe me, fellow-citizens,) the jealousy of a free people ought to be
constantly awake; since history and experience prove, that foreign

influence is one of the most baneful foes of Republican Government. But that jealousy, to be useful, must be impartial; else it becomes the instrument of the very influence to be avoided, instead of a defence against it. Excessive partiality for one foreign nation, and excessive dislike of another, cause those whom they actuate to see danger only on one side, and serve to veil and even second the arts of influence on the other. Real patriots, who may resist the intrigues of the favorite, are liable to become suspected and odious; while its tools and dupes usurp the applause and confidence of the people, to surrender their interests.

36 The great rule of conduct for us, in regard to foreign nations, is, in extending our commercial relations, to have with them as little political connexion as possible. So far as we have already formed engagements, let them be fulfilled with perfect good faith. Here let us stop.

37 Europe has a set of primary interests, which to us have none, or a very remote relation. Hence she must be engaged in frequent controversies, the causes of which are essentially foreign to our concerns. Hence, therefore, it must be unwise in us to implicate ourselves, by artificial ties, in the ordinary vicissitudes of her politics, or the ordinary combinations and collisions of her friendships or enmities.

38 Our detached and distant situation invites and enables us to pursue a different course. If we remain one people, under an efficient

government, the period is not far off, when we may defy material injury from external annoyance; when we may take such an attitude as will cause the neutrality, we may at any time resolve upon, to be scrupulously respected; when belligerent nations, under the impossibility of making acquisitions upon us, will not lightly hazard the giving us provocation; when we may choose peace or war, as our interest, guided by justice, shall counsel.

39 Why forego the advantages of so peculiar a situation? Why quit our own to stand upon foreign ground? Why, by interweaving our destiny with that of any part of Europe, entangle our peace and prosperity in the toils of European ambition, rivalship, interest, humor, or caprice?

40 It is our true policy to steer clear of permanent alliances with any portion of the foreign world; so far, I mean, as we are now at liberty to do it; for let me not be understood as capable of patronizing infidelity to existing engagements. I hold the maxim no less applicable to public than to private affairs, that honesty is always the best policy. I repeat it, therefore, let those engagements be observed in their genuine sense. But, in my opinion, it is unnecessary and would be unwise to extend them.

41 Taking care always to keep ourselves, by suitable establishments, on a respectable defensive posture, we may safely trust to temporary alliances for extraordinary emergencies.

42 Harmony, liberal intercourse with all nations, are recommended by policy, humanity, and interest. But even our commercial policy should hold an equal and impartial hand; neither seeking nor granting exclusive favors or preferences; consulting the natural course of things; diffusing and diversifying by gentle means the streams of commerce, but forcing nothing; establishing, with powers so disposed, in order to give trade a stable course, to define the rights of our merchants, and to enable the government to support them, conventional rules of intercourse, the best that present circumstances and mutual opinion will permit, but temporary, and liable to be from time to time abandoned or varied, as experience and circumstances shall dictate; constantly keeping in view, that it is folly in one nation to look for disinterested favors from another; that it must pay with a portion of its independence for whatever it may accept under that character; that, by such acceptance, it may place itself in the condition of having given equivalents for nominal favors, and yet of being reproached with ingratitude for not giving more. There can be no greater error than to expect or calculate upon real favors from nation to nation. It is an illusion, which experience must cure, which a just pride ought to discard.

43 In offering to you, my countrymen, these counsels of an old and affectionate friend, I dare not hope they will make the strong and lasting impression I could wish; that they will control the usual current of the passions, or prevent our nation from running the course, which has hitherto marked the destiny of nations. But, if I may even flatter

myself, that they may be productive of some partial benefit, some occasional good; that they may now and then recur to moderate the fury of party spirit, to warn against the mischiefs of foreign intrigue, to guard against the impostures of pretended patriotism; this hope will be a full recompense for the solicitude for your welfare, by which they have been dictated.

44 How far in the discharge of my official duties, I have been guided by the principles which have been delineated, the public records and other evidences of my conduct must witness to you and to the world. To myself, the assurance of my own conscience is, that I have at least believed myself to be guided by them.

45 In relation to the still subsisting war in Europe, my Proclamation of the 22d of April 1793, is the index to my Plan. Sanctioned by your approving voice, and by that of your Representatives in both Houses of Congress, the spirit of that measure has continually governed me, uninfluenced by any attempts to deter or divert me from it.

46 After deliberate examination, with the aid of the best lights I could obtain, I was well satisfied that our country, under all the circumstances of the case, had a right to take, and was bound in duty and interest to take, a neutral position. Having taken it, I determined, as far as should depend upon me, to maintain it, with moderation, perseverance, and firmness.

47 The considerations, which respect the right to hold this conduct, it is not necessary on this occasion to detail. I will only observe, that, according to my understanding of the matter, that right, so far from being denied by any of the Belligerent Powers, has been virtually admitted by all.

48 The duty of holding a neutral conduct may be inferred, without any thing more, from the obligation which justice and humanity impose on every nation, in cases in which it is free to act, to maintain inviolate the relations of peace and amity towards other nations.

49 The inducements of interest for observing that conduct will best be referred to your own reflections and experience. With me, a predominant motive has been to endeavour to gain time to our country to settle and mature its yet recent institutions, and to progress without interruption to that degree of strength and consistency, which is necessary to give it, humanly speaking, the command of its own fortunes.

50 Though, in reviewing the incidents of my administration, I am unconscious of intentional error, I am nevertheless too sensible of my defects not to think it probable that I may have committed many errors. Whatever they may be, I fervently beseech the Almighty to avert or mitigate the evils to which they may tend. I shall also carry with me the hope, that my Country will never cease to view them with indulgence; and that, after forty-five years of my life dedicated to its

service with an upright zeal, the faults of incompetent abilities will be consigned to oblivion, as myself must soon be to the mansions of rest.

51 Relying on its kindness in this as in other things, and actuated by that fervent love towards it, which is so natural to a man, who views it in the native soil of himself and his progenitors for several generations; I anticipate with pleasing expectation that retreat, in which I promise myself to realize, without alloy, the sweet enjoyment of partaking, in the midst of my fellow-citizens, the benign influence of good laws under a free government, the ever favorite object of my heart, and the happy reward, as I trust, of our mutual cares, labors, and dangers.

George Washington

United States - September 17, 1796

THOMAS JEFFERSON

I never submitted the whole system of my opinions to the creed of any party of men whatever, in religion, in philosophy, in politics, or in anything else, where I was capable of thinking for myself. Such an addiction is the last degradation of a free and moral agent.

~ Thomas Jefferson, Letter to Francis Hopkinson (March 13, 1789). In: Merrill D. Peterson (ed.), Letters of Thomas Jefferson, New York, 1984, pp. 940-42. [PL Ford, Writings of Thomas Jefferson, vol. 5, pp. 75-78].

The happiness of society depends so much on preventing party spirit from infecting the common intercourse of life, that nothing should be spared to harmonize and amalgamate the two parties in social circles.

~ Thomas Jefferson, To William C. Claiborne, July 1801

You will soon find that so inveterate is the rancor of party spirit among us, that nothing ought to be credited but what we hear with our own ears. If you are less on your guard than we are here, at this moment, the designs of the mischief-makers will not fail to be accomplished, and brethren and friends will be made strangers and enemies to each other,

~ Thomas Jefferson, To James Monroe, March 1808

I deplore with you the putrid state into which our newspapers have passed, and the malignity, the vulgarity, and mendacious spirit of those who write for them. … This has in a great degree been produced by the violence and malignity of party spirit.

~ Thomas Jefferson, To Walter Jones, Jan. 1814

ALEXANDER HAMILTON

Nothing could be more ill-judged than that intolerant spirit which has, at all times, characterized political parties.

~ Alexander Hamilton, The Federalist #1, October 27, 1787.

We are attempting, by this Constitution, to abolish factions, and to unite all parties for the general welfare.

~ Alexander Hamilton, Debates in the Convention of the State of New York on the Adoption of the Federal Constitution, Tuesday, June 25, 1788. In: Henry Cabot Lodge, ed., The Works of Alexander Hamilton (Federal Edition), Vol. 2, New York, 1904, p. 57.

JAMES MADISON

A zeal for different opinions concerning religion, concerning government, and many other points, as well of speculation as of practice; an attachment to different leaders ambitiously contending for pre-eminence and power; or to persons of other descriptions whose fortunes have been interesting to the human passions, have, in turn, divided mankind into parties, inflamed them with mutual animosity, and rendered them much more disposed to vex and oppress each other than to co-operate for their common good.

~ James Madison, The Federalist #10, November 22, 1787

So strong is this propensity of mankind to fall into mutual animosities, that where no substantial occasion presents itself, the most frivolous and fanciful distinctions have been sufficient to kindle their unfriendly passions and excite their most violent conflicts.

~ James Madison, The Federalist #10, November 22, 1787

<!–

Among the numerous advantages promised by a well constructed Union, none deserves to be more accurately developed than its tendency to break and control the violence of faction.

~ James Madison, The Federalist #10, November 22, 1787

"The whole modern world has divided itself into Conservatives and Progressives. The business of Progressives is to go on making mistakes. The business of Conservatives is to prevent mistakes from being corrected."

— G.K. Chesterton

The following Guide to ballot access has been reprinted with the permission of the National Association of Secretaries of State.

NASS
National Association
of Secretaries of State

SUMMARY: STATE LAWS REGARDING PRESIDENTIAL BALLOT ACCESS FOR THE GENERAL ELECTION
SEPTEMBER 2012

This document provides a summary of the laws in each state relevant to the placement of a candidate for president on the general election ballot, and the requirements for a presidential candidate to run as a write-in candidate. Generally a presidential candidate nominated by a political party that meets certain criteria is placed on the general election ballot. This criterion is often based on a threshold number of votes cast at a recent election for a particular office or offices. A number of states provide an alternative mechanism for an organization to qualify in order to nominate candidates, for example by filing a petition or having a certain number of voters affiliated with the organization. Additionally, all states have a procedure for independent candidates, and in some cases individual presidential candidates of a political organization, to obtain ballot access. Most states also permit a presidential candidate to be a write-in candidate, and many of these states require that the candidate file a notice prior to the election.

The summary for each state includes the timeframes for certifying the names of the candidates for president and vice-president and the names of the presidential electors; the requirements for a political party to be eligible to nominate a presidential candidate; the number of signatures required on a petition in order for a presidential candidate to obtain ballot access; a description of any additional ballot access methods where applicable; and the timeframes required for filing a notice in order to be a write-in candidate for president.

It is important to note that the information in this document is based on a NASS review of relevant state ballot access requirements. This document is intended to provide a general overview of these requirements. It is not intended as an interpretation of those laws, or as a procedure guide or manual for political parties or prospective candidates with regard to presidential ballot access. States have a variety of filings and other requirements pertaining to political parties, presidential candidates, presidential electors, and petitions. Additionally, ballot access laws may change at any time based on new state laws and/or court decisions. Candidates and political parties should contact the relevant state election office and/or legal counsel for information on the specific rules and requirements for each state. Additionally, where political parties nominate a candidate, the nomination process varies greatly based on the state, the legal status of each party, and the rules and procedures of each party. Individuals should contact the political parties for information on the party nomination process.

Alabama
Political Party Nomination

A presidential candidate nominated by a political party may be placed on the general election ballot. A political party must certify to the secretary of state no later than {September 6th} the name of the candidates for president and vice-president and the names of the presidential electors. A political party is an organization of electors which received more than 20% of the entire vote cast in the state at the last general election. An organization may also qualify as a political party by filing with the secretary of state on the date of the first primary election a petition containing the number of signatures equal to or exceeding 3% of electors who cast ballots for the office of governor in the last general election.

Petition

An independent candidate for president may obtain ballot access for the general election by filing with the secretary of state {no later than September 6th } a petition containing the signatures of at least 5,000 qualified electors. The petition must be accompanied by a list of presidential electors.

Write-In

In all non-municipal elections a voter may write-in the name of any person not included on the ballot.
(Alabama Code §§ 17-6-22, 17-6-27, 17-6-28, 17-6-29, 17-13-40, 17-13-50, 17-14-31).

Alaska
Political Party Nomination

A presidential candidate nominated by a recognized political party may be placed on the general election ballot. A recognized political party must certify to the division of elections no later than the 48th day prior to the election the name of the candidates for president and vice-president. The political party must certify to the director of election no later than {September 1st} (September 4th in 2012) the names of the party's nominees for presidential electors. A recognized political party is an organized group of voters whose candidate for governor in the last general election received at least 3% of the votes cast for that office, or whose number of registered voters is equal to at least 3% of the total votes cast for governor at the last general election. If the office of governor was not on the ballot at the preceding general election but the office of United States Senate was, the 3% threshold applies to that office.

If neither the office of governor nor the office of United States Senator was on the ballot, the 3% threshold applies to the office of United States Representative.

A limited political party may be organized for the purpose of selecting candidates for presidential electors by filing with the director of elections at least 90 days before a presidential election a petition signed by a number of qualified voters equal to at least 1% of the number of votes cast for president at the last presidential election.

Independent Candidate Petition

An independent candidate for president may obtain ballot access for the general election by filing with the director of elections no later than the 90th day before a presidential election a petition containing the signature of qualified voters equal to at least 1% of the number of votes cast for president at the last general election. The candidates must certify to the director of elections no later than {September 1st} the name of the candidates for president and vice-president and the names of the presidential electors.

Write-In

A write in candidate for president must file a letter of intent with the director of elections at least 5 days before the general election.

(Alaska Statutes §§ 15-25-105, 15.30.020, 15.30.025; 15.30.026; 15.80.010).

Arizona
Political Party Nomination

A presidential candidate nominated by a recognized political party may be placed on the general election ballot. Each recognized political party must file with the secretary of state no less than 90 days before the primary election the names of the party's nominees for presidential electors.

A recognized political party is a political organization that received at least 5% of the total votes cast for governor or presidential electors at the last preceding general election, or a political organization entitled to continued representation by having registered voters equal to at least 2/3 of 1% of the total number of registered voters in the state.

A political organization may also become eligible for recognition as a political party by filing with the secretary of state no less than 140 days before the primary election, or no less than 75 days prior to the presidential preference election, a petition containing the signatures of at least 1 and 1/3% of the total votes cast for governor at the last preceding general election. The petition must include signatures from electors in at least 5 different counties, and at least 10% of the signatures must be from electors in counties with populations less than 500,000.

Petition

A presidential candidate who is not a member of a recognized political party may obtain ballot access for the general election by filing with the secretary of state no less than 60 days before the general election nomination papers and a petition containing the number of signatures equal to 3% of the registered voters in the state. The petition must include the names of the presidential electors. Each of the electors must also file nomination papers.

Write-In

A write-in candidate for president must file nomination papers with the secretary of state no later than the 40th day prior to the election. Each of the presidential electors must also file nomination papers.

(Ariz. Rev. Stat. §§ 16-243, 16-244, 16-312, 16-341, 16-344, 16-801, 16-803,16-804).

Arkansas
Political Party Nomination

A presidential candidate nominated by a political party may be placed on the general election ballot. A political party must certify to the secretary of state no later than {September 15th} the names of the presidential electors.

A political party is a group of voters whose candidate for governor or nominee for presidential electors at the last preceding general election received at least 3% of the entire vote cast for the office. A new political party may be formed by filing with the secretary of state no later than 45 days before the preferential primary election a petition containing the signatures of at least 10,000 registered voters in the state.

Petition

A presidential candidate of a political group may obtain ballot access for the general election by filing with the secretary of state no later than the first Monday of August a petition containing the names of 1,000 qualified electors. The group must file with the secretary of state no later than the 75th day before the election a certificate stating the names of the candidates for president and vice-president and must certify to the secretary of state no later than {September 15th} a list of presidential electors.

An independent presidential candidate may obtain ballot access for the general election by filing with the secretary of state no later than the first Monday in August a petition containing the names of 1,000 qualified electors and certifying to the secretary of state no later than September 15th a list of the presidential electors.

(Ark. Code Ann. §§ 7-1-101, 7-5-525, 7-7-205, 7-8-302).

California
Political Party Nomination

A presidential candidate nominated by a qualified political party may be placed on the general election ballot. A qualified political party generally must certify to the secretary of state no later than {October 1st} the names of the presidential electors.

A qualified political party is a political party that received for any of its candidates for statewide office at the last preceding gubernatorial election at least 2% of the entire vote statewide. A group may also qualify as a political party if on or before the 135th day before any primary election a number of registered voters equal to at least 1% of the entire vote of the state at the last gubernatorial election are affiliated with the party; or, if it files with the secretary of state no later than 135 days prior to the primary election a petition signed by the number of voters equal to at least 10% of the entire vote of the state at the last gubernatorial election.

Petition

An independent presidential candidate may obtain ballot access for the general election by filing with county election officials no later than 88 days before the election a declaration of candidacy for each of the presidential electors and nomination papers signed by the number of voters equal to at least 1% of the entire number of registered voters in the state. The nomination papers must include the name of the presidential electors, and may include the name of the candidates for president and vice-president.

Write-In

A write-in candidate for president must have each of the presidential electors file a declaration of write-in candidacy with the secretary of state no later than 14 days before the election. **(California Elections Code Ann. §§ 338, 5001, 5100, 6901, 7100, 7110, 7300, 7578, 7843, 8303, 8304, 8400, 8403(a)(2), 8451, 8550, 8650,8651, 8652, 8653).**

Colorado
Political Party Nomination

A presidential candidate nominated by a major or minor political party may be placed on the general election ballot. Political parties must file with the secretary of state no later than 60 days before the general election a certificate of nomination for presidential electors. The name of the presidential candidate may be added to the certificate.

A major political party is a political party that that was represented on the ballot at the last preceding gubernatorial election by a political party candidate or individual nominee who received at least 10% of the total gubernatorial votes cast.

A minor political party is a political party that had a candidate for statewide office in either of the last two preceding general election and received at least 1% of the total votes cast for any statewide office, or has 1,000 or more registered electors affiliated with the party prior to {July 1st} in either of the last two preceding general elections.

A political party may also qualify as a minor political party through any of the following methods:

the party had a candidate for statewide office in either of the last two preceding general elections and received at least five percent of the total votes cast for such office; one thousand or more registered electors are affiliated with the minor political party prior to {July 1st} of the election year for which the minor party seeks to nominate candidates; or the party files with the secretary of state no later than the {second Friday of January} a petition containing the signatures of 10,000 registered electors.

Petition

An unaffiliated presidential candidate may obtain ballot access for the general election by filing with the secretary of state no later than the 155th day before the election a petition containing the signatures of at least 5,000 eligible electors and a notice of acceptance of the nomination from the presidential candidate and each of the electors.

Fee

An unaffiliated presidential candidate may obtain ballot access for the general election by filing with the secretary of state no later than

155 days before the election a statement of intent and a $500 fee.

Write-In

A presidential write-in candidate must file with the secretary of state an affidavit of intent no later than the 110th day prior to the election.

(Colo. Rev. Stat. §§ 1-1-104, 1-3-100.3, 1-4-302, 1-4-303, 1-4-502; 1-4-701, 1-4-802; 1-4-1101, 1-4-1102, 1-4-1302, 1-4-1303, 1-4-130)

Connecticut
Political Party Nomination

A presidential candidate nominated by a major or minor political party may be placed on the general election ballot. Political parties must file with the secretary of state no later than the 14th day after the close of the state convention the names of the nominees for presidential electors. A minor political party must certify the names of nominees to the secretary of state no later than the 62nd day prior to the election.

A major political party is a political party whose candidate for governor at the last preceding election for governor received at least 20% of the whole number of votes cast for all candidates for governor, or, whose enrolled membership is at least 20% of the total number of enrolled members of all political parties in the state.

A minor political party is a political party whose candidate for the office in question received at the last preceding regular election at least 1% of the whole number of votes cast for all candidates for that office.

Petition

A presidential candidate who does not receive a nomination from a minor or major political party may obtain ballot access for the general election by filing with the secretary of state no later than the 90th day prior to the election a petition containing the number of signatures of qualified electors equal to the lesser of 1% of the votes cast for the office at the last election, or 7,500. The names of the presidential electors must be included on the petition. The names of the candidates for president and vice-president must be filed with the secretary of state at the time a petition form is requested.

Write-In
A presidential write-in candidate must register with the secretary of state and submit the names of the presidential electors no later than 4:00 pm of the 14th day preceding the election.
(Conn. Gen. Stat. §§ 9-175, 9-372, 9-388, 9-452, 9-453b, 9-453d, 9-453i).

Delaware
Political Party Nomination
A presidential candidate nominated by a qualified political party may be placed on the general election ballot. Each eligible political party must file with the state election commissioner no later than {September 1st} a certificate of nomination that includes the name of the candidates for president and vice-president and the names of the presidential electors. If a party holds a national nominating convention, the certificate must be filed by the earlier of the Tuesday following the convention, or {September 15th}.

A political party is a political organization which nominates candidates for presidential electors, or nominates candidates for offices to be decided at the general election. A political party is eligible for general election ballot access if 21 days prior to the primary election the number of registered voters in the name of the party is equal to at least 10/100 of 1% of the total number of voters registered in the state as of {December 31st} of the year immediately preceding the general election.

Petition
An unaffiliated presidential candidate may obtain ballot access for the general election by filing with the state election

commissioner no later than {September 1st} a sworn declaration of non-affiliation and a nominating petition signed by at least 1% of the total number of registered voters as of {December 31st} of the year immediately preceding the general election.

Write-In
A write-in candidate for president must file a write-in candidate declaration with the state election commissioner no later than {September 30th}.
(Del. Code Ann. tit. 15, §§ 101, 3001, 3002, 3301, 3303, 3402).

Florida
Political Party Nomination
A presidential candidate nominated by a political party may be placed on the general election ballot. The governor must nominate the presidential electors for each political party and certify the names of the electors to the department of state no later than {September 1st}. A minor political party affiliated with a national party holding a nominating convention must certify to the department of state no later than September 1st the names of the candidates for president and vice-president and the names of the presidential electors.

A minor political party is any group which on {January 1st} preceding a primary election does not have registered as members 5% of the total registered electors of the state.

Petition
An unaffiliated presidential candidate, and a presidential candidate of a minor political party that is not affiliated with a national party holding a nominating convention, may obtain ballot access for the general election by filing with the department of state no later than {July 15th} a petition signed by 1% of the registered electors of the state. The party or candidate must file with the department of

state no later than {September 1st} the names of the presidential electors.

Write-In

A write-in candidate for president must file an oath with the department of state and must certify the names of the presidential electors no later than the 49th day prior to the primary election in the presidential election year.

(Fla. Stat. §§ 97.021, 103.021, 103.022).

<u>Georgia</u>

Political Party Nomination

A presidential candidate nominated by a political party or a political body may be placed on the general election ballot. Political bodies that nominate presidential electors by convention must hold the convention at least 150 days prior to the general election, or, in years following the release of a decennial census, 120 days before the election.

A political party is a political organization that nominated a candidate for governor at the last general election and the candidate received at least 20% of the votes cast in the state for that office; or nominated a candidate for president at the last presidential election and the candidate received at least 20% of the vote cast for that office.

A political body is any political organization other than a political party. A political body is eligible to nominate candidates for the general election by convention if the political body nominated a candidate for statewide office at the preceding general election and the candidate received the number of votes equal to at least 1% of the total number of registered voters for that election; or, if the political body files with the secretary of state no later than the second Tuesday in July a petition signed by the number of voters equal to 1% of the registered voters in the preceding general election. In a general election year following the release of a decennial census, the petition must be filed no later than the first Monday in August. A presidential candidate nominated by a political body must file a notice of candidacy no later than the Friday following the fourth Monday in June. In a general election year following the release of a decennial census, the notice of candidacy must be filed no later than the Friday following the last Monday in July.

Petition

An independent presidential candidate, or a presidential candidate of a political body, presidential candidate may obtain ballot access for the general election by submitting to the secretary of state no later than no later than the second Tuesday in July a nominating petition signed by the number of voters equal to 1 percent of the total number of registered voters eligible to vote in the last presidential election. In a general election year following the release of a decennial census, the petition must be filed no later than the first Monday in August.

The candidate must file with the secretary of state no later than the Friday following the fourth Monday in June a notice of candidacy and a qualifying fee equal to 3% of the annual fee of the office. In a general election year following the release of a decennial census, the notice of candidacy and qualifying fee must be filed no later than the Friday following the last Monday in July.

Write-In

A write-in candidate must file intention of write-in candidacy with the secretary of state no later than the Tuesday after the first Monday in

September prior to the election and must publish notice of the candidacy in a newspaper of general circulation.
(Ga. Code Ann. §§ 21-2-2, 21-2-130, 21-2-131, 21-2-132, 21-2-133, 21-2-170, 21-2-172, 21-2-180, 21-2-185, 202-187, 21-2-285)

Hawaii
Political Party Nomination

A presidential candidate nominated by a qualified political party may be placed on the general election ballot. Qualified political parties must file with the chief election officer no later than the 60th day prior to the election a certification of the party's nominees for electors, and a sworn application that includes the name of the party's candidates for president and vice-president and a statement that the candidate is the chosen candidate of both the state and national party. A national party is one that is admitted to the ballot in at least one state other than Hawaii or one which is determined by the chief election officer to be making a bona fide effort to become a national party. If there is no national party or the national and state parties do not agree on the presidential candidate, the chief election officer may determine which candidate's name shall be placed on the ballot or may leave the candidate's name off the ballot.

A qualified political party is an association of voters which had candidates running for election at the last general election for any of the statewide offices whose terms had expired, and the party received: at least 10% of all votes cast for any statewide office or in at least 50% of the congressional districts, or; at least 4% of the votes cast for all the offices of state senator statewide, or; at least 4% of the votes cast for all the office of state representative statewide, or; at least 2% of the votes cast for all the offices of state senate and all the offices of state representative combined statewide

A group of persons may qualify as a political party by filing with the chief state election officer no later than the 170th day before the next primary election a petition containing the signatures of at least 1/10 of 1% of the total registered voters in the state as of the last preceding election.
Petition

An individual presidential candidate or the presidential candidate of a party our group that is not a qualified political party may obtain ballot access for the general election by filing with the chief election officer no later than the 90th day prior to the general election a petition containing the signatures of at least 1% of the number of votes cast in the state at the last presidential election.

(H.R.S. §§ 11-61b, 11-62, 11-113, 14-21)

Idaho
Political Party Nomination

A presidential candidate nominated by a political party may be placed on the general election ballot. Each political party must certify to the secretary of state no later than {September 1st} the names of the candidates for president and vice-president and the names of the presidential electors, unless a 5 day extension is granted by the secretary of state.

A political party is an organization of electors that had 3 or more candidates for state or national office listed under the party name at the last general election, or had a candidate for state or national office at the last general election receive at least 3% of the aggregate vote cast for governor or presidential electors. An affiliation of new electors may form a new political party by filing with the secretary of state no later than {August 30th} in even numbered years a petition containing the signatures of qualified electors equal to at least 2% of the aggregate vote cast for presidential electors in the state at the previous general election at the last presidential election.

Petition

An independent presidential candidate may obtain ballot access for the general election by filing with the secretary of state no later than

August 25th prior to the election a petition signed by 1,000 qualified electors. The candidate must file with the secretary of state no later than September 1st the names of the presidential electors.

Write-In
A write-in candidate for president must file a declaration of intent with the secretary of state no later than 28 days before the election.
(Idaho Code §§ 34-501, 34-702, 34-708A , 34-711; 34-711A)

Illinois
Political Party Nomination
A presidential candidate nominated by an established political party may be placed on the general election ballot. Each established political party must certify to the state board of election within 2 days of the state nominating convention the names of the party's nominees for presidential electors.

An established political party is a political party whose candidate for governor at the last general election for state and county offices received more than 5% of the entire vote cast for governor. A political party that received more than 5% of the entire vote cast in the state at the general election next preceding a primary is also an established political party.

Petition
An independent presidential candidate, or a presidential candidate of a new political party, may obtain ballot access for the general election by filing with the state board of elections no less than 134 prior to the election a petition signed by 1% of the number of voters who voted at the next preceding statewide general election or 25,000 qualified voters, whichever is less. The petition must include the names of the presidential electors.

Write-In

A write-in candidate for president must file a declaration of intent with the each county clerk and board of commissioners in the state no later than 61 days prior to the election.
(10 Ill. Comp. Stat. §§5/7/2, 5/7-9, 5/10-2, 5/10-3, 5/10-6, 5/17-16.1, 5/18-9.1)

Indiana
Political Party Nomination

A presidential candidate nominated by a major political party or other qualified political party may be placed on the general election ballot. Political parties must certify to the elections division no later than the second Tuesday in September the names of the nominees for president and vice-president and the names of the nominees for presidential electors A major political party refers to either of the two political parties whose nominee for secretary of state in the last election received the highest and second highest number of votes statewide for that office. A political party also qualifies to nominate candidate for presidential electors if its nominee for secretary of state at the last election received at least 2% of the total votes cast for that office.

Petition

An independent presidential candidate or a presidential candidate of a minor political party not qualified to nominate by convention may obtain ballot access for the general election by filing with the elections division no later than {July 15th} a written consent form and a petition containing the signatures of registered voters equal to 2% of the votes cast at the last election for secretary of state. The name of the candidates for president and vice-president and the names of presidential electors must be filed with the secretary of state no later than the second Tuesday in September.

Write-In

A write-in candidate for president must file a declaration of intent with the division of elections no later than July 3rd prior to the election.
(Ind. Code §§ 3-5-2-26.6, 3-5-2-30, 3-8-2-2.5, 3-8-2-4, 3-8-2-5, 3-8-4-1, 3-8-4-2, 3-8-4-10, 3-8-6-10, 3-8-6-12, 3-10-4-1, 3-10-4-5)

Iowa
Political Party Nomination

A presidential candidate nominated by a political party may be placed on the general election ballot. Political parties must certify to the secretary of state no later than the 81st day before the election the names of the candidate for president and vice-president and the names of the presidential electors. If the national nominating convention of a political party adjourns later than 89 days before the general election the names of the candidates for president and vice-president must be certified within 5 days after adjournment. As an alternative to certification by the state central committee of the political party, the certificate of nomination issued by the political party's national nominating convention may be used to certify the name of the party's candidates for president and vice-president.

A political party is a party whose candidate for president at the last presidential election, or candidate for governor at the last gubernatorial election, received at least 2% of the total vote cast for all candidate for that office at that election.

A political organization that is not a political party may hold a convention or caucus to nominate a presidential candidate if a minimum of 250 eligible electors attend, including at least one from each county. The organization must certify to the secretary of state no later than the 81st day before the election the name of the candidates for president and vice-president, the names of the presidential electors, and the names of the delegates in attendance at the convention or caucus.

Petition

An independent presidential candidate, or a presidential candidate of a political organization that does not hold a nominating caucus or convention, may obtain ballot access for the general election by filing with the secretary of state no later than the 81st day before the election an affidavit of candidacy and a petition signed by at least 1500 eligible electors residing in at least 10 counties of the state. The filing must include the names of the presidential electors.

Write-In

A voter may write-in the name of a candidate.
(Iowa Code §§ 44.1, 44.2, 43.2, 44.4, 44.17, 45.1 ,45.4, 49.99, 54.5)

Kansas
Political Party Nomination

A presidential candidate nominated by a recognized political party may be placed on the general election ballot. Recognized political parties must certify to the secretary of state the names of the presidential electors. The certification may also include the names of the candidates for president and vice-president.

A recognized political party is a political party which nominates a person for at least one statewide office at any general election, and whose nominee for any statewide office receives at least 1% of the votes cast for the office at the election. A political party may obtain official recognition by filing with the secretary of state no later than {June 1st} prior to the primary election a petition containing the signatures of at least 2% of the total votes cast for all candidates for the office of governor in the state in the last preceding general election.

Petition

An independent presidential candidate may obtain ballot access for the general election by filing with the secretary of state no later than the Monday preceding the primary election a petition signed by at least 5,000 qualified voters. The petition must include the name of the candidates for president and vice-president and the names of the presidential electors. The candidate must file with the secretary of state an affidavit of candidacy no later than the 2nd Monday preceding the general election.

Write-In
A write-in candidate for president must file an affidavit of intent with the secretary of state no later than the second Monday preceding the election.
(Kan. Stat. Ann. §§ 25-202, 25-301, 25-302a, 302b, 25-303, 25-304, 25-305, 25-305b, 25-804)

Kentucky
Political Party Nomination
A presidential candidate nominated by a political party or political organization may be placed on the general election ballot. Each political party or political organization must certify to the secretary of state no later than the Friday following the first Tuesday in September the name of the presidential candidate and the names of the presidential electors.

A political party is an organization of electors whose candidate received at least 20% of the total vote cast at the last preceding election for presidential electors. A political organization is a group not constituting a political party whose candidate received 2% or more of the vote at the last preceding election for presidential electors.

Petition

An independent presidential candidate, a political group presidential candidate, and a presidential candidate of a political organization not entitled to nominate by convention, may obtain ballot access for the general election by filing with the secretary of state no later than the Friday following the first Tuesday in September a nominating petition signed by at least 5,000 registered voters. The petition must include the names of the presidential electors.

Write-In

A write-in candidate for president must file a declaration of intent and a list a presidential electors with the secretary of state no later than the fourth Friday in October preceding the election.

(Ky. Rev. Stat. Ann. §§ 117.265, 118.015, 118.305, 118.315, 118.325, 118.365)

Louisiana
Political Party Nomination

A presidential candidate nominated by a recognized political party may be placed on the general election ballot. Each recognized political party must file with the secretary of state the names of the presidential electors. If the nominees for president and vice-president and the names of the presidential electors are not certified to the secretary of state by the state central committee of the political party no later than the first Tuesday in September, the national chairman of the party must certify the names of the presidential electors to the secretary of state no later than the first Friday following the first Tuesday in September.

A political party may qualify as a recognized political party if at least 1,000 registered voters are registered as affiliated with the party ninety days prior to the opening of the qualifying period; or, if any candidate of the party for presidential elector at the last presidential election received at least 5% of the votes cast or any candidate of the party for any statewide office in any primary or general election received at least 5% of the votes cast for the office.

Petition

An independent presidential candidate may obtain ballot access for the general election by filing with the secretary of state no later than the first Friday following the first Tuesday in September a notice of candidacy, affidavit of each elector, and a petition containing at least 5,000 signatures of registered voters, at least 500 of which must be obtained in each of the congressional districts. The petition must include the name of the presidential candidate and the names of the presidential electors.

Fee

An independent presidential candidate may obtain ballot access for the general election by paying a $500 fee and filing notice of the presidential electors.

(Louisiana Rev. Statutes §§18-441, 18:464(A), 18-465, 18-1253, 18-1254, 18-1255)

Maine
Political Party Nomination

A presidential candidate nominated by a qualified political party may be placed on the general election ballot. Each qualified political party nominates presidential electors. A qualified political party is a party that was listed on the ballot at either of the 2 preceding general elections and had at least 10,000 voters enrolled in the party voted in the last general election.

A political party may also qualify if it had a candidate for governor or for president in the last preceding general election, who was nominated by petition, receive 5% or more of the total votes cast in the state for governor or for president, or; 10 or more voters not enrolled in a qualified political party file with the secretary of state on the 180th day before the primary election a petition containing the signatures of voters equal in number to at least 5% of the total vote cast in the state for governor at the last preceding gubernatorial election.

Petition

A presidential candidate that is not nominated by a political party may obtain ballot access for the general election by filing with the secretary of state no later than {August 15th} a petition signed by at least 4,000 and not more than 6,000 voters. The petition must include the names of the candidates for president and vice-president and the names of the presidential electors.

Write-In

A write-in candidate for president must file a declaration of write-in candidacy with the secretary of state no later than the 45th day prior to the election.
(21-A Me. Rev. Stat. Ann. §§ 301, 302, 303, 321, 351, 354)

Maryland
Political Party Nomination

A presidential candidate nominated by a qualified political party may be placed on the general election ballot. Qualified political parties must certify to the state board of elections no later than {September 6th} the names of the candidates for president and vice-president and must certify with the state board of election no later than 30 days before the general election the names of the presidential electors.

A qualified political party is a political party that has nominated a candidate for the highest office on the ballot in a statewide general election and the candidate received at least

1% of the total vote for that office, or; if state voter registration totals as of {December 31st} show that at least 1% of the state's registered voters are affiliated with the political party.

A group of voters may form a new qualified political party by filing with the state board of election no later than the first Monday in August containing the signatures of at least 10,000 registered voters.

Petition

A presidential candidate that is not affiliated with a political party may obtain ballot access by submitting a petition with the state board of election no later than the first Monday in August a certificate of candidacy and a petition containing the signatures of at least 1% of the registers voters of the state. The candidate must certify to the state board of election no later than 30 days before the election the names of the presidential electors.

Write-In

A write-in candidate for president must file a certificate of candidacy with the state board of elections no later than the Wednesday before the election.
(Md. Ann. Code Art. 33, §§ 1-101, 4-102, 4-103, 5-301, 5-303, 5-701, 7-503, 5-704, 8-503)

Massachusetts
Political Party Nomination

A presidential candidate nominated by a political party may be placed on the general election ballot. Each political party must certify to the secretary of state no later than the second Tuesday of September the names of the candidates for president and vice-president and the names of the presidential electors.

A political party is any party whose candidate for any statewide office at the last general election received at least 3%

of the vote cast for that office, or, a party with a number of enrolled voters equal to or greater than 1% of the entire voters registered in the state.

Petition

A presidential candidate not running as the candidate of a political party may obtain ballot access by submitting to the secretary of state no later than the second Tuesday of September nomination papers containing the signatures of at least 10,000 voters. The nomination papers must include the names of the candidates for president and vice-president and the names of the presidential electors.

Write-In

A write-in candidate for president must file the name of the candidate for president and the names of the candidates for presidential electors with the secretary of state no later than 60 days prior to the election.

(Mass. Gen. Laws §§ 50-1, 53-1, 53-6, 53-8, 53-10, 54-78A)

Michigan
Political Party Nomination

A presidential candidate nominated by a political party that qualifies for general election ballot access may be placed on the general election ballot. Each political party must certify to the secretary of state no later than 1 business day after the conclusion of the state convention the names of the candidates for presidential electors. Each political party must certify to the secretary of state not more than 1 business day after the state or national convention of the party, whichever is later, the names of the candidates for president and vice-president.

A political party qualifies for ballot access at the general election if any of the party's candidates at the last preceding general election received at least 1% of the total number of votes cast for the successful candidate for the office of secretary of state at the last preceding general election in which a secretary of state was elected.

A group may form a new political party by filing with the secretary of state no later than the 100th day before the general election a petition containing the signatures of registered and qualified electors equal to not less than 1% of the total number of votes cast for all candidates for governor at the last election in which a governor was elected. The petition must be signed by at least 100 registered electors in each of at least 1/2 of the congressional districts of the state.

Petition

A presidential candidate not affiliated with a political party may obtain ballot access for the general election by filing with the secretary of state no later than the 110th day before the election a petition signed by a number of qualified and registered electors of the state equal to not less than 1% of the total number of votes cast for all candidates for governor at the last election in which a governor was elected. [note: see Michigan Secretary of State Ballot Access Information for Presidential Candidates on their website which states that the number of valid signatures required is 30,000]. The petition must be signed by at least 100 registered electors in each of at least 1/2 of the congressional districts of the state. The candidate must certify to the secretary of state no later than 66 days before the election the names of the presidential electors.

Write-In

A write-in candidate for president must file a declaration of intent with the secretary of state no later than the second Friday immediately preceding the election.

(Mich. Comp. Laws §§ 168.16, 168.42, 168.532, 168.544f , 168.560a, 168.590b, 168.590c, 168.590d, 168.591, 168.685, 168.686, 168.686a, 168.737a).

Minnesota
Political Party Nomination

A presidential candidate nominated by a major political party may be placed on the general election ballot. Each major political party must certify to the secretary of state the names of the presidential electors and the names of the candidates for president and vice-president at least 71 days before the general election.

To qualify as a major political party, a political party must meet one of the following requirements: present at least one candidate for constitutional office at the last general election for these offices, or presidential elector or U.S. senator at the last presidential election, who received votes in each county, and received at least 5% of the total votes in that election; or present at least 45 candidates for state representative, 23 candidates for state senator, 4 candidates for representative in Congress, and 1 candidate for each constitutional office, at the last general election for these offices; or file a nominating petition with the secretary of state prior to the close of filing for the state primary containing the signatures of party members that equal at least 5% of the total votes at the last state general election.

Petition

A presidential candidate of a minor political party or other party, and independent presidential candidates, may obtain ballot access by filing with the secretary of state no later than 77 days before the general election a petition containing the signatures of at least 2,000 eligible voters. The petition must include the names of the presidential electors.

A minor political party is a party that presented at least one candidate for constitutional office at the last general election for these offices, or presidential elector or U.S. senator at the last presidential election, who received votes in each county in the aggregate equal to at least

1% of the total number of individuals who voted in the election; or, the party filed with the secretary of state no later than the close of filing for the state primary a nominating petition containing the signatures of party members equal in number to at least 1% of the total number of individuals who voted in the preceding general election.

Write-In

A write-in candidate for president must file a written request to have their write-in votes tallied and the names of the presidential electors with the secretary of state no later than the 7th day before the election.

(Minn. Stat. §§ 200.02, 204B.07, 204B.08, 204B.09, 208.03)

Mississippi
Political Party Nomination

A presidential candidate nominated by an organized political party may be placed on the general election ballot. Each political party must certify the names of the presidential electors to the secretary of state no less than 60 days prior to the election.

Petition

An independent presidential candidate may obtain ballot access by filing with the secretary of state no less than 60 days before the election a petition containing the signatures of 1,000 qualified electors. The petition must be accompanied by the names of the individual who will serve as presidential electors.

Write-In

A write-in vote will be counted in the event of the death, resignation, withdrawal, or removal of any candidate whose name was printed on the official ballot

(Miss. Code. Ann. §§ 23-15-365, 23-15-539, 23-15-781, 23-15-785, 23-15-1063)

Missouri
Political Party Nomination

A presidential candidate nominated by an established political party may be placed on the general election ballot. Each established political party must certify the names of its nominees for president and vice-president to the secretary of state no later than the 12th Tuesday prior to the election, or within 7 working days after choosing its nominee for president, whichever is later. Each established political party must certify to the secretary of state no later than the 3rd Tuesday prior to the election, the names of its nominees for presidential elector.

To qualify as an established political party, a political party's candidate for statewide office at either of the last two general elections must have received more than 2% of the entire vote cast for the office.

A group may form a new political party and nominate a presidential candidate to be placed on the general election ballot if the group files with the secretary of state no later than the 15th Monday immediately preceding the general election a petition containing the signatures of at least 10,000 registered voters. The petition must include the names of the nominees for presidential electors and the name of the presidential candidate.

Petition

An independent presidential candidate may obtain ballot access for the general election by filing with the secretary of state no later than the 15th Monday immediately preceding the general election a declaration of candidacy and petition containing the signatures of at least

10,000 registered voters. The petition must include the names of the presidential electors and the names of the candidates for president and vice-president.

Write-In

A write-in candidate for president must submit a declaration of intent and the names of the nominees for presidential electors with the secretary of state no later than the second Friday immediately preceding the election.
(MO. Rev. Stat. §§ 115.013,, 115.315, 115.317, 115.321, 115.329, 115.399, 115-453)

Montana
Political Party Nomination
A presidential candidate nominated by a qualified political party may be placed on the general election ballot. Each qualified political party must certify to the secretary of state by the date prescribed by the secretary of state the names of the nominees for presidential electors.

A political party is qualified if it had a candidate for a statewide office in either of the last two general elections and received 5% or more of the total votes cast for the most recent successful candidate for governor. A political party may also qualify by filing with the secretary of state no later than 85 days before the date of the primary a petition containing the number of signatures of registered voters equal to 5% or more of the votes cast for the successful candidate for governor at the last general election, or 5,000 electors, whichever is less. The number must include the registered voters in more than 1/3 of the legislative districts equal to 5% or more of the total votes cast for the successful candidate for governor at the last general election in those districts or 150 electors in those districts, whichever is less.

Petition
An independent presidential candidate or a presidential candidate of a political party that does not qualify may obtain ballot access for the general election by filing with the secretary of state 76 days prior to the general election a petition

containing the signatures of electors equal to 5% or more of the total votes cast for the successful candidate for governor at the last general election, or 5,000 electors, whichever is less. The names of the candidates and presidential electors must be certified to the secretary of state no later than 76 days before the election

Write-In

A presidential write-in candidate for president must submit a declaration of intent with the secretary of state no later than the 10th day before absentee ballots must be made available
(Mont. Code. Ann. §§ 13-10-504, 13-10-601, 13-25-101, 13-10-211)

Nebraska
Political Party Nomination

A presidential candidate nominated by a political party that meets state requirements for partisan ballot access may be placed on the general election ballot. The officers of the various national political party conventions must certify to the secretary of state no later than {September 8th} the names of the candidates for president and vice-president. Each political party must hold a state convention no later than {September 1st} to select presidential electors and must certify the names of the electors to the secretary of state.

A political party meets state requirements for partisan ballot access if a candidate nominated by the political party at one of the two immediately preceding statewide general elections received at least 5% of the vote in a statewide race, or if a combination of candidates nominated by the political party for a combination of districts that encompass all of the voters of the entire state polled at least 5% of the vote in each of their respective districts.

Petition

Presidential candidates of a newly formed political party, and nonpartisan presidential candidates, may obtain ballot access for the general election by filing with the secretary of state no later than {September 1st} a petition containing the signatures of at least 2500 registered voters who did not vote in the primary election of any political party that held a presidential preference primary election. The petition must include the names of the candidates for president and vice-president and the names of the presidential electors.

A group may form a new political party by filing with the secretary of state no later than August 1st a petition containing signatures equal to at least 1% of the total votes cast for governor at the most recent general election for that office. The petition signatures must be distributed to include registered voters totaling at least 1% of the votes cast in the most recent gubernatorial election in each of the 3 congressional districts in the state.

Write-In

A write-in candidate for president must file an affidavit of intent and the required filing fee with the secretary of state no later than 10 days prior to the election.

(Neb. Rev. Stat. §§ 32-610, 32-615, 32-617, 32-620, 32-621, 32-710, 32-712, 32-716, 32-813)

Nevada
Political Party Nomination

A presidential candidate nominated by a qualified major or minor political party may be placed on the general election ballot. Each major and minor party must certify the names of the presidential electors to the secretary of state. A minor party must certify to the secretary of state no later than the first Tuesday in September the names of the candidates for president and vice-president.

To qualify as a major political party: the party must be designated as a political party on the voter registration applications of at least 10% of the registered voters. the state on January 1st preceding any primary election, or; the party must file a petition with the secretary of state no later than the last Friday in February before any primary election containing the signatures of registered voters equal to or more than 10% of the total number of votes cast at the last preceding general election for the office of representative in congress.

To qualify as a minor political party: any of the party's candidates for partisan office at the last general election must have received at least 1% of the total number of the total votes cast for the office of representative in congress; on January 1st preceding a primary election, the party must have been designated as the political party on the voter registration applications of at least 1% of the total number of registered voters in the state; or the party must file a petition with the secretary of state no later than the 3rd Friday in May preceding the general election containing the signatures of registered voters equal to at least 1% of the total number of votes cast at the last preceding general election for the office of representative in congress.

Petition

An independent presidential candidate may obtain ballot access for the general election by filing with the secretary of state no later than the second Friday in August a declaration of candidacy, a filing fee of $250, and a petition containing the signatures of registered voters equal to at least 1% of the total number of votes cast at the last preceding general election for the office of representative in congress. The candidate must also file with the secretary of state the names of the individuals who will serve as presidential electors.

(Nev. Rev. Stat. §§ 293.128, 293.270, 293.1715, 293.1725, 298.020, 298.109)

New Hampshire
Political Party Nomination

A presidential candidate nominated by a political party may be placed on the general election ballot. Each political party must certify to the secretary of state no later than the last Tuesday of October the names of the presidential electors.

A political party is any political organization which received at least 4% of the total number of votes cast for governor or United States senators at the preceding state general election.

A political organization may also nominate a presidential candidate for the general election by filing with the secretary of state no later than the Wednesday one week before the primary nomination papers containing the signatures of registered voters equal to 3% of the votes cast at the previous state general election. The name of the candidate and a declaration of candidacy must be submitted to the secretary of state no later than the day of the primary.

Petition

A presidential candidate may obtain ballot access for the general election by filing a declaration of intent between the first Wednesday in June and the Friday of the following week, and submitting to the secretary of state no later than the Wednesday one week before the primary nomination papers containing the signatures of 3,000 registered voters, 1,500 from each United States congressional district in the state. The candidate must also pay a fee of $250.

Write-In

A voter may write-in the name of a candidate on the ballot.

(N.H. Rev. Stat. Ann. §§ 652:11, 655:40a, 655:40b, 655:42, 655:43, 655:53, 655:54, 659:17, 667:21)

New Jersey
Political Party Nomination

A presidential candidate nominated by a political party may be placed on the general election ballot. Political parties must certify the names of the presidential electors to the secretary of state within 1 week after the electors are nominated at a state convention which must be held within 1 week following the closing of the party's national convention. The certificate may include the names of the candidates for president and vice-president.

A political party is a party which, at the election held for all of the members of the general assembly next preceding the holding of any primary election, polled for members of the general assembly of at least 10% of the total vote cast in the state.

Petition

A presidential candidate who is not nominated by a political party, and independent presidential candidate, may obtain ballot access for the general election by filing a petition with the secretary of state no later than the 99th day before the general election a petition containing the signatures of 800 legally qualified voters of the state. The names of the presidential electors may be included in the petition.

Write-In

A voter may write-in the name of a candidate.

(N.J. Stat. Ann. §§19:1-1, 19:5-1, 19:13-2, 19:13-1, 19:13-3, 19:13-4, 19:13-5, 19:13-9, 19:13-15, 19:53A5)

New Mexico

Political Party Nomination

A presidential candidate nominated by a qualified political party may be placed on the general election ballot. A qualified political party must certify the names of the presidential electors to the secretary of state no less than 56 days prior to the election.

A qualified political party is a political party that has a candidate on the ballot in at least one of the two previous general elections, or if the party has a candidate for governor or president in a general election, the candidate receives at least 1% of the total votes cast for the office.

A political party may qualify as a political party by filing with the secretary of state petition containing the signatures of at least ½ of 1% of the total votes cast for the office of governor at the preceding general election.

Petition

An independent presidential candidate may obtain ballot access for the general election by filing with the secretary of state on the 21st day following the primary election a declaration of candidacy and a nominating petition containing the number of voter signatures equal to at least 3% of the total vote cast for governor at the last preceding general election for that office. The petition must include the names of the presidential electors.

Write-In

A write-in candidate must file a declaration of intent with the secretary of state no later than the 21st day after the primary election.

(N.M. Stat. Ann. §§ 1-1-10, 1-7-2, 1-8-1, 1-8-49, 1-8-51, 1-8-52, § 1-12-19.1, 1-15-3)

New York

Political Party Nomination

A presidential candidate nominated by a political party may be placed on the general election ballot. Political parties must certify to the state board of elections no later than 14 days after the fall primary election the names of the nominees for presidential electors.

A political party is any political organization whose candidate for governor at the last preceding election for that office received at least 50,000 votes.

Petition

An independent presidential candidate may obtain ballot access for the general election by filing with the state board of elections no later than 11 weeks prior to the election a petition containing 15,000 signatures, with at least 100 signatures coming from each of ½ of the congressional districts in the state. The petition must include the names of the presidential electors. The candidate must file an acknowledgment of acceptance of the nomination no later than the 3rd day after the last day to file the petition.

Write-In

A write-in candidate for president must file a certificate of candidacy and a list of presidential electors with the state board of elections no later than the third Tuesday before the general election.

(N.Y. Election Law §§ 1-104, 6-102, 6-142, 6-146, 6-153, 6-158)

North Carolina

Political Party Nomination

A presidential candidate nominated by a political party may be placed on the general election ballot. Political parties must certify the names of the presidential electors with the secretary of state. A political party is any group whose candidate for governor or presidential electors at the last preceding general election received at least 2% of the entire vote cast in the state for governor or presidential electors.

A group may form a new political party by filing with the state board of election no later than the 1st day of June preceding the general election a petition containing the number of signatures of registered voters equal to 2% of the total number of voters who voted in the most recent general election for governor. The petition must be signed by at least 200 registered voters from each of the 4 congressional districts in the state.

Petition

An unaffiliated presidential candidate may obtain ballot access for the general election by filing with the state board of elections no later than the last Friday in June preceding the general election a petition containing the number signatures of registered voters equal to 2% of the total number of voters who voted in the most recent general election for governor. The petition must be signed by at least 200 registered voters from each of the 4 congressional districts in the state. The candidate must certify to the secretary of state no later than the first Friday in August the name of the candidate for vice-president and the names of the presidential electors.

Write-In

A write-in candidate for president must file with the state board of election no later than 90 days before the election a declaration of intent and a petition containing the signatures of 500 qualified voters.

(N.C. Gen. Stat. §§ 163-1, 163-96, 163-122, 163-123, 163-209, 163-213)

North Dakota
Political Party Nomination

A presidential candidate nominated by an established political party may be placed on the general election ballot. Established political parties must certify to the secretary of state no later than the 60th day before the election the names of the presidential electors and the names of the candidates for president and vice-president. An established political party is a political organization that had candidates for presidential electors, a candidate for governor, a candidate for attorney general, or a candidate for secretary of state on the last general election ballot and the candidates received at least 5% of the total vote cast for the office.

Petition

A presidential candidate of a party that is not established, or an independent presidential candidate, may obtain ballot access for the general election by filing with the secretary of state no later than the 60th day before the general election an affidavit of candidacy, a statement of interests, and a petition containing the signatures of 4,000 qualified electors. The names of the presidential electors must be filed with the petition.

Write-In

A write-in candidate for president must file a certificate of write-in candidacy and the names of the presidential electors with the secretary of state no later than the 21st day before the election

(N.D. Cent. Code §§ 16.1-03-14, 16.1-03-19, 16.1-06-07.1, 16.1-12-02, 16.1-12-02.2)

Ohio
Political Party Nomination

A presidential candidate nominated by a political party may be placed on the general election ballot. Major political parties must certify to the secretary of state on or before the 90th day before the election names of the candidates for president and vice-president. Major parties must nominate presidential electors no later than 40 days prior to the general election and must certify the names of the electors to the secretary of state within 5 days. Minor parties must certify to the secretary of state on or before the 90th day before the election the names of the candidates for president and vice-president and the names of the presidential electors.

A political party is any party whose candidate for governor or nominees for presidential elector at the most recent general election received at least 5% of the entire vote cast for that office.

A group may also obtain political party status by petition (Ohio Secretary of State http://www.sos.state.oh.us/)

Petition

An independent presidential candidate may obtain ballot access for the general election by filing with the secretary of state no later than the 90th day before the general election a petition containing the signatures of at least 5,000 qualified electors. The candidate must file a statement of candidacy and the names of presidential electors with the petition.

Write-In

A write-in candidate for president must file a declaration of intent and a list of presidential electors with the secretary of state no later than the 72nd day before the election.
(Ohio Rev. Code Ann. §§ 3505.10, 3513.11, 3513.041, 3513.257, 3517.01)

Oklahoma
Political Party Nomination

A presidential candidate nominated by a recognized political party may be placed on the general election ballot. Each recognized political party must certify to the state board of elections no fewer than 90 days from the date of the general election the names of the nominees for presidential electors.

A recognized political party is a political party whose nominee for governor or nominees for presidential electors received at least 10% of the total votes cast for the office in any general election. A group may form a recognized political party by file with the state elections board any time except between March 1st and November 15th of an even numbered year a petition containing the signature of registered voters equal to at least 5% of the total votes cast in the last general election for governor or for presidential electors.

etition

Uncommitted candidates for presidential electors may obtain ballot access for the general election by filing a petition with the state elections board no later than July 15th of a presidential election year containing the signatures of registered voters equal to at least 3% of the total votes cast in the last general election for president.

An independent presidential candidate, or a presidential candidate nominated by an unrecognized political party, may obtain ballot access for the general election by filing with the state elections board no later than July 15th of a presidential election year a petition containing the signatures of registered voters equal to at least 3% of the total votes cast in the last general election for president. The candidate must certify to the state board of elections no later than {September 1st} the name of the candidate for vice-president and the names of the presidential electors.
(Oklahoma Statutes §§ 26-1-108, 26-1-109, 26-10-101, 26-10-101.1, 26-10-101.2)

Oregon
Political Party Nomination
A presidential candidate nominated by a major or minor political party may be placed on the general election ballot. Political parties must certify to the secretary of state no later than the 70th day before the election the names of the candidates for president and vice-president and the names of the presidential electors.

A political party qualifies as a major political party if a number of electors equal to at least 5% of the number of registered electors in the state are registered as members of the party no later than the 275th day before the date of a primary election. A political party qualifies as a minor political party if: an affiliation of electors files with the secretary of state no later than two years after filing a prospective a petition a petition containing the signatures of electors equal to 1 ½ % of the total votes cast for all candidates for governor at the most recent election at which a candidate governor was elected to a full term; the candidate of an affiliation of electors receives at least 1% of the total votes cast for presidential electors at the last presidential election, or receives 1% of the votes cast for any state offices for which nominations by political parties are permitted at the most recent election for those offices.

Petition

A non-affiliated presidential candidate may obtain ballot access for the general election by filing with the secretary of state no later than the 70th day before the general election a petition containing the signatures of individual electors equal to, not less than, 1% of the total votes cast for all candidates for presidential electors at the last general election. The names of the presidential electors must be filed with the petition.

Assembly of Electors

A non-affiliated presidential candidate may obtain ballot access for the general election through nomination by an assembly of at least 1,000 electors gathered in one place for no longer than 12 hours. The signatures of the assemble members and a certificate of nomination must be filed with the secretary of state no later than the 70th day before the general election. The names of the presidential electors must be filed with the certificate of nomination.

Write-In

A voter may write-in the name of a presidential candidate.
(Or. Rev. Stat. Ann. §§ 248.006, 248.008, 248.315, 248.355, 249.705, 249.722, 249.735, 249.740, 254.500, 254.548)

Pennsylvania
Political Party Nomination

A presidential candidate nominated by a political party may be placed on the general election ballot. The nominee of each political party must certify to the secretary of the commonwealth within thirty days after the national convention of the party the names of the presidential electors.

A political party is any party or political body whose candidates at the general election next preceding the primary received in each of at least ten counties in the state no less than 2% of the largest entire vote cast in each of the counties for any elected candidate, and received a total vote in the state equal to at least 2% of the largest entire vote cast in the state for any elected candidate.

Petition

Presidential candidates of minor parties and political bodies may obtain ballot access for the general election by filing with the secretary of the commonwealth no later than the 2nd Friday subsequent to the primary an affidavit of candidacy, a $200 fee and nomination papers containing the signatures of qualified electors equal to at least 2% of the largest entire vote cast for any elected candidate in the state at the last preceding election at which statewide candidates were voted for.

A minor political party is a party whose statewide registration is less than 15% of the combined statewide registration for all statewide political parties and otherwise meets the criteria of a political party. A political body which is not a political party but has nominated candidates by nomination papers is a political body.

Write-In

A voter may write-in the name of a presidential candidate on the ballot.

(Pa. Consol. Stat. Ann. §§ 2831, 2878, 2872.2, 2873, 2911, 2913, 2914, 3031.12)

Rhode Island
Political Party Nomination

A presidential candidate nominated by a political party may be placed on the general election. Political parties must nominate presidential electors at a meeting to be held no later than {October 14th}.

A political party is any political organization that: nominated a candidate for governor at the next preceding general election for general officers who received at least 5% of the entire vote cast for governor, or; nominated a candidate for president at the next preceding presidential election who received at least 5% of the entire vote cast in the state for president. A political organization may also obtain political party status by filing with the local boards of canvassers no later than {August 1st} petition forms containing the signatures of registered qualified voters equal to 5% of the entire vote cast in the state for governor or president in the immediately preceding general election.

Petition

An independent presidential candidate or presidential candidates seeking to establish a political party may obtain ballot access by filing nomination papers containing the signatures of 1000 voters. The candidate must file a declaration of candidacy, and, where applicable, a notice of intent to establish a political party, no later than the last day for filing with the secretary of state for congressional and statewide offices. The nomination papers must be filed with local boards of election no later than 60 days before the election.

Write-In

A voter may write-in the name of a presidential candidate on the ballot.

(R.I. Gen. Laws §§ 17-1-2, 17-12-13, 17-12-15, 17-14-7, 17-14-11, 17-14-12, 17-19-31)

South Carolina
Political Party Nomination

A presidential candidate nominated by a political party may be placed on the general election ballot. Political parties nominate presidential electors, and must certify names of the candidates for president and vice-president to the state election commission no later than {September 10th}.

A political party is a political party, organization, or association certified by the state election commission. An organization may obtain certification as a political party by filing with the state election commission no later than 6 months prior to the election a petition containing the signatures of 10,000 or more registered electors.

Petition

A presidential candidate may obtain ballot access for the general election by filing with the state election commission no later than July

15th a petition containing the signatures of at least 5% of qualified registered electors, provided that the petition candidate is not required to furnish more than 10,000 signatures. The names of the presidential electors must be filed with the secretary of state.

Write-In

Write-in votes for president are not allowed.
(S.C. Code Ann. §§ 7-7-120, 7-9-10, 7-9-90, 7-11-10, 7-11-70, 7-13-320, 7-13-350, 7-13-351, 7-13-360, 7-19-70).

South Dakota
Political Party Nomination

A presidential candidate nominated by a political party may be placed on the general election ballot. The chairperson of the national convention of each political party must certify to the secretary of state immediately following the convention the names of the candidates for president and vice-president. If the national certification is not received, the names must be certified by the state chairperson of the party at the request of the secretary of state. Each political party must certify to the secretary of state the nominees for presidential electors within three days of the state convention, and no later than the 2nd Tuesday in August.

A political party is a party whose candidate for governor at the last preceding general election for governor received at least 2 ½ percent of the total votes cast for governor.

A new political party may be formed by filing with the secretary of state no later than the last Tuesday of March prior to the date of the primary election a written declaration signed by at least 2 ½ percent of the voters in the state as shown by the total vote cast for governor at the last preceding gubernatorial election.

Petition

An independent presidential candidate may obtain ballot access for the general election by filing with the secretary of state no later than the first Tuesday in August prior to the election a certificate of nomination containing the number of signatures equal to at least 1% of the total combined vote cast for governor at the last certified gubernatorial election. The candidate must file a declaration of candidacy and certify the name of a candidate for vice-president prior to circulation the nominating petition.

(S.D. Codified Laws §§ 12-1-3, 12-5-3.16, 12-5-1, 12-5-21, 12-5-22, 12-7-7)

Tennessee
Political Party Nomination

A presidential candidate nominated by a statewide political party or a minor political party may be placed on the general election ballot. Candidates nominated by political parties must be immediately certified to the coordinator of elections.

A statewide political party is a political party that had at least 1 candidate for an office to be elected by voters of the entire state in the past 4 years who received a number of votes equal to at least 5% of the total number of votes cast or gubernatorial candidate in the most recent election for governor.

A minor political party may obtain ballot access for the general election by filing a petition no later than 90 days prior to the general election with the coordinator of elections containing the signature of registered voters equal to at least 2.5% of the total number of votes cast for gubernatorial candidates in the most recent election for governor.

Petition

An independent presidential candidate may obtain ballot access by filing with the coordinator of elections no later than the 3rd Thursday in August a petition containing the signatures of 25 or more registered voters for each elector allotted to the state, which totals 275 valid signatures. The candidate must also file the names of the presidential electors and the Vice Presidential nominee.

Write-In

Write-in candidates must file a notice with the appropriate election official no later than 50 days before the election, and must also submit elector information.
(Tenn. Code. Ann. §§ 2-1-104, 2-5-101, 2-7-133, 2-13-201, 2-13-203, § 2-1-104(a)(31)(a), (a)(24), 2-13-107(a), 2-5-101(a)(1), 2-15-101, 2-15-102, 2-7-133(i); 2012 Tenn. Pub. Acts ch. 55)

Texas
Political Party Nomination

A presidential candidate nominated by a political party may be placed on the general election ballot. Political parties must certify the names of the candidates for president and vice-president and the names of the presidential electors before the later of the 70th day before the presidential election, or the first business day after the date of final adjournment of a party's national nominating convention.

A political party that is authorized or required to nominate candidates by primary election is entitled to have its nominee for president placed on the general election ballot. A political party is authorized to nominate by primary if the party's nominee for governor in the most recent gubernatorial general election received at least 2% of the total number of votes received by all candidates for governor in the election; a political party is required to nominate by primary if that candidate received more than 20% of the vote. A political party that nominates candidates by convention is entitled to have its nominee for president placed on the general election ballot if the party had a nominee for statewide office at the last general election receive a number of votes equal to at least 5% of the total number of voters received by all candidates for that office.

A political party that nominates by convention may also qualify to place a presidential candidate on the general election ballot if the party files with the secretary of state no later than the 75th day after precinct conventions a list convention participants indicating that the number of participants equals at least 1% of the total number of votes received by all candidates for governor in the most recent gubernatorial general election. If the number of convention participants is fewer than the number required, the party may qualify for ballot access at the general election by filing a petition with secretary of state containing a number of signatures that when added to the number of convention participants on the list equals at least 1% of the total number of voters received by all candidates for governor in the most recent gubernatorial election.

Petition

An independent presidential candidate may obtain ballot access for the general election by filing with the secretary of state no later than the 2nd Monday in May an application and a petition containing the number of signatures equal to at least 1% of the total vote received in the state by all candidates for president in the most recent presidential election. The application must include the names of the presidential electors.

Write-In

A write-in candidate for president must file a declaration of write-in candidacy and the names of the presidential electors with the secretary of state no later than the 78th day before the election.

(Tex. Elections Code Ann. §§ 146.023, 146.025, 172.002, 181.005, 181.006, 192.003, 192.032, 192.033)

Utah

Political Party Nomination

A presidential candidate nominated by a registered political party may be placed on the general election ballot. Each registered political party must certify the names of the candidates for president and vice-president to the lieutenant governor no later than {August 31st}, or provide written authorization for the lieutenant governor to accept the certification a candidate for president from the national office of the registered party. Each registered party must certify to the lieutenant governor no later than {August 31st} the names of the presidential electors.

To qualify as a registered political party an organization must have participated in the last general election and in at least one of the last two regular general elections received for any of its candidates for any office a total vote equal to 2% or more of the total votes cast for all candidates for the united states house of representative in the same election.

An organization may also become a registered political party by filing with the lieutenant governor on or before {February 15th} of the year in which a regular general election will be held a petition containing the signatures of at least 2,000 registered voters. If a newly registered political party does not hold a national party convention the party may designate the names of its candidate for president and the names of the presidential electors to the lieutenant governor by {August 15th}.

Petition

An independent presidential candidate may obtain ballot access for the general election by filing with the lieutenant governor no later than August 15th a certificate of nomination, a nominating petition containing the signatures of 1,000 registered voters, and a $500 fee.

Write-In

A write-in candidate for president must file a declaration of write-in candidacy with the lieutenant governor no later than 30 days before the election.

(Utah Code Ann. §§ 20A-8-101, 20A-8-103, 20A-8-106, 20A-9-202, 20A-9-502, 20A-9-503, 20A-9-601, 20A-13-301)

Vermont
Political Party Nomination

A presidential candidate nominated by a major political party may be placed on the general election ballot. Major political parties must certify the names of the presidential electors promptly after the electors are nominated at a party convention held no later than the 4th Tuesday in September. The parties must certify to the secretary of state no later than the 47th day before the general election the names of the party's nominee for president and vice-president.

A presidential candidate may be nominated by a minor political party and placed on the general election ballot if the party has town committees organized in at least 10 towns in the state and files a statement of nomination with the secretary of state no later than the second Thursday after the first Monday in June preceding the primary election.

Petition

An independent presidential candidate may obtain ballot access for the general election by filing with the secretary of state no later than the second Thursday after the first Monday in June preceding the primary election a statement of nomination containing the signatures of

1,000 registered voters and a consent form from each nominee for presidential elector.

Write-In

A voter may write-in the name of a presidential candidate on the ballot.

(Vt. Stat. Ann. tit. 17, §§ 2103, 2319, 2356, 2381, 2382, 2385, 2386, 2387, 2402, 2587, 2403, 2716, 2721, 2722)

Virginia
Political Party Nomination

A presidential candidate nominated by a political party may be placed on the general election ballot. Each political party must provide to the state board of elections no later than the 74th day before the election the names of the presidential electors selected at the party's convention and the names of the candidates for president and vice-president. A political party whose national convention is scheduled to be held after the 74th day before the election must file with the state board of election no later than the 74th day before the election the certification of the presidential electors and a certification of the persons expected to be nominated for president at its national convention. The party must certify the names of the candidates for president and vice-president nominated at the national party convention no later than the 60th day before the election.

A political party is an organization which received at least 10% of the total vote cast for any statewide office at either of the two preceding statewide general elections.

Petition

A group of qualified voters not constituting a political party may obtain ballot access for a presidential candidate by filing with the state board of elections no later than the 74th day before the election a petition containing the signatures of at least 10,000 qualified voters including signatures of at least 400 qualified voters from each congressional district. The petition must include the names of the candidates for president and vice-president and the names of the presidential electors.

Write-In

A write-in candidate for president must file a declaration of intent with the state board of elections no later than 10 days before the election.

(Va. Code Ann. §§ 24.2-101, 24.2-542, 24.2-542.1, 24.2-543, 24.2-614, 24.2-644)

Washington
Political Party Nomination

A presidential candidate nominated by a major political party may be placed on the general election ballot. Each major political party must certify to the secretary of state at least 50 days before the election the names of the party's nominees for presidential electors and the names of the candidates for president and vice-president.

A major political party is a political party that had at least one nominee for president, vice president, united state senator, or a statewide office receive at least 5% of the total vote cast at the last preceding state general election.

Petition/Assembly

A presidential candidate that is not nominated by a major political party, including minor party candidates and independent candidates, may be placed on the general election ballot by holding an organized assembly attended by at least one hundred registered voters no later than the second Saturday in May or during the first Saturday in June through the fourth Saturday in July. The candidate must file with the secretary of state no later than one week after the convention is held a petition containing the signatures of at least 1,000 registered voters and certificate of nomination, and must file with the secretary of state no later than ten days after the convention is held a list of presidential electors.

Write-In

A write-in candidate for president must file a declaration of write-in candidacy with the secretary of state no later than 18 days before the election.

(**Wash. Rev. Code §§ 29A.04.097, 29A.04.086, 29A.20.111, 29A.20.121, 29A.20.131, 29A.20.141, 29A.20.151, 29A.20.161, 29A.20.181, 29A.24.311, 29A.56.320, 29A.56.360, 29A.80.020**).

West Virginia
Political Party Nomination

A presidential candidate nominated by a political party may be placed on the general election ballot. Political parties nominate the candidates for presidential electors at a state convention in June, July, or August and must certify the names of the electors to the secretary of state within fifteen days.

A political party is an organization whose candidate for governor at the last preceding general election received at least 1% of the total number of votes cast for all candidates in the state for that office.

Petition

A group of citizens that is not a political party (minor party and independent candidates) may obtain ballot access for a presidential candidate by filing with the secretary of state no later than August 1st preceding the general election a certificate of nomination containing the number of signatures of registered voters equal to at least 1% of the entire vote cast for president in the last preceding presidential election. The candidates for president and vice president must also pay a fee equivalent to 1% of the annual salary of the office, provided that the filing fee for president or vice president must not exceed $2500.

Write-In

A write-in candidate for president must file a certificate of announcement with the secretary of state no later than the close of business on the 49th day before the election.
(W. Va. Code §§ 3-1-8, 3-5-8, 3-5-21, 3-5-23, 3-5-24, 3-6-4a)

Wisconsin
Political Party Nomination

A presidential candidate nominated by a recognized political party may be placed on the general election ballot.

Each recognized political party must certify to the general accountability board no later than the first Tuesday in September preceding a presidential election the names of the candidates for president and vice-president. Each recognized party must hold a convention on the first Tuesday in October prior to the presidential election for the purpose of nominating presidential electors and the names of the electors must be immediately certified to the general accountability board.

A recognized political party is a political party whose candidate for any statewide office at the last gubernatorial election received at least 1% of the total votes cast for that office, and if the last general election was also a presidential election, the party's candidate received at least 1% of the total vote cast for that office.

A political organization may also become a recognized political party by filing with the general accountability board no later than April 1st in the year of the partisan primary a petition containing the signatures of at least 10,000 electors, including at least 1,000 electors residing in each of at least 3 separate congressional districts.

Petition

An independent presidential candidate may obtain ballot access for the general election by filing with the general accountability board no later than the first Tuesday in August preceding the partisan primary nomination papers containing between 2,000 and 4,000 signatures. The nomination papers must include the names of the candidates for president and vice-president and the names of the presidential electors.

Write-In

A write-in candidate for president must file a declaration of candidacy and a list of presidential electors with the general accountability board no later than the 2nd Tuesday preceding the election.

(Wis. Stat. §§ 5.02, 5.62, 5.64, 8.16, 8.18, 8.185, 8.20)

Wyoming
Political Party Nomination

A presidential candidate nominated by a major or minor political party may be placed on the general election ballot. The political parties must nominate presidential electors at a state convention and certify the names of the electors to the secretary of state no later than 30 days following termination of the state convention.

A major political party is a political organization whose candidate for united state representative, governor, or secretary of state, received not less than 10% of the total votes cast for that office in the most recent general election. A minor political party is a political organization whose candidate for united states representative, governor, or secretary of state received not less than 2% nor more than 10% of the total votes cast for that office in the most recent general election.

A group may form a new political party and obtain ballot access for the general election by filing with the secretary of state no later than June 1st in a general election year a petition containing the signatures of registered electors equal in number to no less than 2% of the total number of votes cast for the office of united state representative in the last general election.

Petition

An independent presidential candidate may obtain ballot access for the

general election by filing with the secretary of state no later than 70 days before a general election a petition containing the signatures of registered electors numbering not less than 2% of the total number of votes cast for united states representative in the last general election. The petition must be accompanied by a $200 fee.

Write-In

A write-in candidate must file an application of candidacy and the required fee with the appropriate filing officer no later than 2 days after the election.

(Wyo. Stat. Ann. §§ 22-1-102, 22-4-118, 22-4-120, 22-4-303, 22-4-306, 22-4-402, 22-5-101, ,22-5-208, 22-5-301, 22-5-304, 22-5-306, 22-5-307)

www.ingramcontent.com/pod-product-compliance
Lightning Source LLC
Chambersburg PA
CBHW050129280326
41933CB00010B/1303